The Great American MEATLOAF CONTEST™

COOKBOOK

COOKBOOK

GREAT MEATLOAF RECIPES BY GREAT AMERICANS

Featuring Meatloaf, Poultry Loaf, and Vegetarian Loaf Recipes from the Most Recent Contests

Peter "Meatloaf" Kaufman and T. K. Woods

HEARST BOOKS • NEW YORK

It is the policy of William Morrow and Company, Inc., and its imprints and affiliates, recognizing the importance of preserving what has been written, to print the books we publish on acid-free paper, and we exert our best efforts to that end.

Library of Congress Cataloging-in-Publication Data

Kaufman, Peter, 1959–
    The great American meatloaf contest cookbook : featuring meatloaf, poultry loaf, and vegetarian loaf recipes from the most recent contests / by Peter "Meatloaf" Kaufman and T. K. Woods.
        p.   cm.
    Includes index.
    ISBN 0-688-12646-4
    1. Meat loaf.   I. Woods, T. K., 1959–   . II. Title.
    TX749.K38   1994
    641.8'24—dc20   93-28806
                                                                                  CIP

Printed in the United States of America

        5   6   7   8   9   10

BOOK DESIGN BY GIORGETTA BELL MC REE

This book is dedicated to Charlotte Willour, an enlightened and gifted teacher of fourth and fifth graders, Ridge School, Arlington Heights, Illinois, who made me promise I would write a book someday. It's not exactly what we envisioned when I was ten years old, Miss Willour, but life is full of surprises except for the promises we keep.

And thanks to the two best ingredients in my life . . .

my mother, Patricia Woods, who introduced me to the world of cooking and encouraged in me the wonder of creating; and

my father, Lyle Woods, who taught me that diligence, the power of perseverance and steadfast commitment can make anything happen.

T. K. WOODS

I'd like to thank my parents, Roberta and Stuart, my brother, Jeff, and my sister, Susan—four people who didn't laugh when I told them about joining the Great American Meatloaf Contest.

Special thanks to my grandparents, Herman and Faye Kaufman, for always being there for all of us, and my late grandparents, Henry and Shirley Albert, still here in spirit.

I'd also like to thank the members of the following rock groups whose music I'll still be listening to when they wheel me off to the rest home: Mott the Hoople (they broke up in 1975, but I'm still hoping for a reunion), the Boomtown Rats, the Alarm, Ultravox, and the Jam.

And to P. G. Wodehouse, the best and funniest writer ever.

PETER M. KAUFMAN

Acknowledgments

We would like to thank the following people who have made the Great American Meatloaf Contest and this book possible.

Chapin Spencer, Maureen McLaughlin, Keli Phelan, Kevin Phelan, Bob Gregson, Joanne Ohms, Andy Shefrin, Mary Lou Shefrin, Bruce Appell, Hank "Flying Digits" Steinberg, Jay Ginewsky, Sharon Moore, and Steven Kantrowitz.

And especially, our two best friends and supporters, Betsy Phelan and Diane Compton.

Thank you also to the charter members of the Meatloaf Tasting Committee: Dawn Bain, Denny Bain, Rosa Werthwein, Wendy Mandel, Janet Schnee, Kirsten Kissmeyer, Nixie Raymond, Susan Farrell, Pat Wallerstein, Jamie Wallerstein, Pam Levy, Eric Nottleson, Lauri Sklar, and Roger Patkin.

Special thanks to Tim Buie for his enthusiasm and unwavering support and for tasting 600 meatloaves. Also, thanks to the Buie family in Kansas City for their great encouragement. And for Kathleen's magic words that proved an effective tonic during the tough times: "Anyone who can create a Meatloaf Contest can do anything." Thank you.

For continuous coverage, thanks to Julie Schwartz and John Gambling.

Thanks to Kathie Lee Gifford and Regis Philbin for putting meatloaf on national television, and producers Barbara Fight and Michael Gelman for making it so much fun.

A special thanks to Bill Adler for recognizing the possibilities and to our editor, Megan Newman, for helping make it happen.

Contents

Introduction

Why *meatloaf*? Why not a book dedicated to America's favorite comfort food! This cookbook has been created by Americans from California to Texas, Michigan to Alabama, Florida to Vermont, and thirty-five other states. Men and women of all ages have shared their favorite meatloaf recipes and anecdotes with us, and we're sharing them with you.

MORE THAN MEATS THE EYE

It's amazing how many varieties of meatloaf recipes we received for the recent Great American Meatloaf contests. But this book also includes many innovative and delicious poultry loaves and vegetarian loaves.

In this book, you'll find meatloaf roll-ups with a variety of fillings; meatloaves with a kick, several with a Southwestern flair; meatloaves with sauces and gravies perfect for a dinner party; and lots of what we refer to as "just like Mom used to make" meatloaves. So, whether you're an accomplished cook or a novice, you'll find recipes here that are both creative and delicious.

We have divided the book into the following chapters:

- **Just Like Mom Used to Make:** These are quick and very easy to make. The average preparation time is under 10 minutes.
- **Like Mom Used to Make—with a Twist:** These recipes embellish basic meatloaf recipes with sauces, gravies, and fillings.
- **Meatloaf Roll-Ups:** These are loaves that have a filling and are then rolled before baking. There are instructions on the best way to do this at the beginning of the chapter.
- **Meatloaves with a Kick:** Spicy loaves were big this year. These loaves can be adapted to be milder, or if you're a spice lover, even hotter.
- **Dinner Party Meatloaves:** You'd be surprised how many people appreciate a good, simple dinner when dining out. There are no bones to stick in their teeth, no question about which fork to use. You can make these fancier meatloaves far enough ahead so you can spend time with your guests, rather than fuss in the kitchen.
- **Poultry Loaves:** Ground turkey and chicken provide the foundation for some flavorful and healthy loaves.
- **Vegetarian Loaves:** With a variety of grains, nuts, and vegetables, these loaves are delicious as either a main course or a side dish.

THE GREAT AMERICAN MEATLOAF CONTEST BEGINS

How did we start the Great American Meatloaf Contest? T. K. and I were working in the marketing department of a culinary institute a few years ago, and at a business function one evening we listened to a group of businessmen talk about their favorite meatloaf recipes. They discussed this comfort food with great enthusiasm, and several claimed that the only meal they knew how to cook was meatloaf. It was unusual to see men in business suits exchanging recipes and challenging each other on whose recipe was better. The seed was planted in T. K.'s mind. She had developed and managed state-wide cooking contests for a variety of food products, but she realized the world was missing one cooking contest—meatloaf.

The Great American Meatloaf Contest started as a Northeast regional cook-off in Hartford, Connecticut, in the fall of 1991. We received hundreds of diverse and delicious recipes. The response was overwhelming. The contest drew national media coverage, which prompted us to start The Great American Meatloaf National Recipe Contest in 1992. Plus we had so much fun we didn't want to work in "real" jobs anymore.

THE CONTEST AND THE RECIPES

All of the recipes in this book were submitted as entries in the recent Great American Meatloaf contests. Many of them are old family recipes that have been passed down through several generations.

The contest entries were judged by food writers, chefs, and meatloaf enthusiasts from all over the country, who selected the best in each category as well as honorable mentions. T. K. and I had nothing to do with the judging. (And pretty much nothing to do with our friends after tasting over 600 meatloaves.)

Whether a recipe won an award or not is not important. What is important is that meatloaf crosses economic and racial boundaries like no other food we can name. Recipes in this book are from every region of the country, from men and women and teenagers as well as folks in their eighties.

The only recipes in the book that were not contest entries are in the "Meatloaves Created by Family, Friends, and the Test Kitchens" chapter. These are recipes that were developed either at World Meatloaf Headquarters (WMHQ) or by family members and friends.

All of the recipes in this book were tested at World Meatloaf Headquarters (a secret location where some of the world's most advanced meatloaf research is conducted). The WMHQ staff has discovered some interesting and time-saving ideas for making meatloaves that will be discussed throughout the book.

MEATLOAF AND MOM

My mother's recipe was passed down from her mother. (Fathers didn't cook in those days. My father still doesn't know where my mom keeps the glasses.) Mom's meatloaf was always served with lumpy mashed potatoes and some kind of green vegetable that our late, great dog Silver was kind enough to take off my hands. Mom's meatloaf was always made in a large, red roasting pan that she still uses to this day. I've adapted her recipe a little, and you can find Mom's Meatloaf on page 282.

MEN AND MEATLOAF

I think there is a genetic reason why men love meatloaf. I have several theories:

- Men grew up eating meatloaf.
- Meatloaf is simple to make.
- Men love it because they can toss it in the refrigerator and then eat it whenever they want it without having to heat it up or even use a plate.
- There are very few dishes to clean.

As a matter of fact, the first meal I ever cooked for a date in college was meatloaf. I chose it because:

1. I love meatloaf (thankfully, she did too).

2. With the cost of dating, I couldn't afford to take her out to dinner very often.

3. I could make it without having to worry too much about complicated cooking directions.

4. Women appreciate it when men take the time to cook dinner for them.

I'm thirty-four now, and these reasons still apply.

MEATLOAF IN THE 1990s

With the welcome death of what I call "foo-foo" food served in fern-filled, arrogant-waiter-laden restaurants (two peas, a baby carrot, and ½ ounce steak for $25), people have returned to good, basic food that is identifiable, relatively inexpensive, and satisfying. Some of the most famous restaurants across the country now feature meatloaf and are thrilled with the demand for this once diner-only entree.

Traditional meatloaf consists of the following basic components: meat, bread crumbs or other binder, and spices and/or herbs. As you'll see in this book, that is the starting point for some incredible creativity.

Reflecting the move toward health-conscious eating in America, we have included poultry and vegetarian loaves. Honestly, I wasn't thrilled when the meatloaf staff insisted on including a vegetarian category in the contest. Faced with the thought of tasting a vegetarian loaf, I tried unsuccessfully to slip into another room at World Meatloaf Headquarters. But I was surprised how good they were! Though I wouldn't serve a vegetarian loaf during Super Bowl half-time, I did serve one once to some unsuspecting carnivores and nothing was left but the crumbs.

During my weekly poker game and meatloaf tastings (that way my poker losses are deductible), some very understanding friends tried a lot of these recipes. Their favorite was the Super Bowl Kielbasa Loaf on page 286. It's a dense, chewy loaf that sticks to your ribs—and probably your arteries, too. But in moderation, it's just about perfect.

YOU CAN'T GO WRONG

What if I don't have a quarter-pinch of saffron? Can I substitute one herb for another without the dish exploding in the oven? To ease your mind, there is not one recipe in this book that includes saffron. And yes, you can substitute two or three herbs for another; you can use fresh or dried; you can stand on your head while cooking if it will make you feel comfortable. That's the whole point about meatloaf: *comfort in cooking as well as eating.*

This is why I love meatloaf so much. With the exception of a few more complicated recipes, most in this book can be made with everyday items. You won't be forced to hunt through the grocery store for an $11 pinch of some foreign spice that you'll never use again.

If a recipe calls for a certain ingredient and you're out of it, be creative! Really, how much can go wrong with a meatloaf?

COLD OR HOT, IT HITS THE SPOT

Does meatloaf taste better the day you cook it, or a day or two later? Personally, I like to cook it one day, let it cool, wrap it in wax paper and aluminum foil, refrigerate it, and eat it a day or two later. The rest gives the flavors a chance to blend. I usually cook two meatloaves at a time and freeze one for later.

I have a friend who loves cold meatloaf sandwiches on white bread with ketchup. He hasn't eaten a hot meatloaf in years and plans to keep it that way.

Whether you're a seasoned cooking professional or a single person just starting out in your first apartment, we hope you will enjoy the recipes, anecdotes, and cooking tips in this book.

Chapter 1

Meatloaf Basics

I *need what?* In cooking a few hundred meatloaves during the past six months, the WMHQ staff discovered one basic rule for cooking: Gather everything you need *before* you start cooking. We assemble all the ingredients on a cookie sheet before we start. That way we can see if we're out of an ingredient before we're halfway through the recipe.

That's just one meatloaf cooking tip. Here are some others.

TIPS FROM WORLD MEATLOAF HEADQUARTERS

Serving size. All the recipes have the suggested number of servings right below the title. *These are approximate.* A rule of thumb is to allow ¼ to ½ pound meat per person. One recipe we received suggested that four pounds of meat serve two people. If you invite these people over for dinner, I'd suggest serving the meatloaf in a trough.

Types of meat. In our testing, we used ground beef that was 80 to 90 percent lean. If you use a fattier meat, it is especially important to use a pan that will allow the meat to drain while cooking. Or pour off the fat several times during cooking. Meatloaf with a higher fat content will also shrink more than leaner beef. Most of the recipes call for lean ground beef.

Some recipes call for a combination of beef, veal, pork, and/or lamb. The veal provides a lighter texture while the pork and lamb add flavor. If you prefer not to use those meats, substitute an equivalent amount of ground beef.

Some of the recipes require ground sirloin. We suggest you do not substitute ground beef for the sirloin because the change will affect the taste as well as the texture and size of the finished loaf.

A WORD ABOUT BREAD CRUMBS

Crumbs. All the recipes in this book use bread crumbs as a basic ingredient. Use the amount given in each recipe as a guide. But depending on how fatty the meat is, or how dry you like your meatloaf, add more bread crumbs a tablespoon at a time until you reach the consistency you want. The loaf should be slightly wet when you put it in the oven.

Bacon for meatloaves. Many recipes call for uncooked bacon to be placed on top of the loaf prior to cooking. A way to decrease the grease is to boil the bacon for 3 minutes. This parboiling extracts some of the fat while still giving the meatloaf a great bacon flavor.

Out of it? Substitute. If a recipe requires an ingredient that you don't have, be creative. Substitute your favorite spice for one you're missing. However, if the recipe calls for ground beef, don't substitute bologna! You won't be very happy.

Pans. We use aluminum meatloaf pans. We cut slits in the bottom of the pan and put the pan on a wire stand (a cooling or roasting rack). We then place the rack on a foil-lined cookie sheet with sides. The fat drains onto the sheet, making cleanup a lot easier.

When making a free-form meatloaf, we suggest the following method:

1. Coat a large piece of aluminum foil with nonstick cooking spray or lightly coat it with vegetable oil.

2. Cut a few slits in the piece of aluminum foil.

3. Shape the loaf and place it on the foil.

4. Place the foil with the meatloaf on a cooling or roasting rack.

5. Place the rack on a foil-lined cookie sheet with sides.

This method will allow you to cook the meatloaf thoroughly, reduce the amount of fat, and have a quick and easy cleanup.

Cooking times. Since no two ovens are calibrated exactly alike, the cooking temperature may vary a little. Also, using a different size pan than the one specified in the recipe may alter the cooking time. Most meatloaves containing 2 to 3 pounds of meat should cook for 1 to 1½ hours. Check the loaf after 1 hour by quickly pressing your finger on the top of the loaf. If the loaf springs back a little, it's done. (Don't let your finger rest too long on the loaf. Skin burns.)

As an alternative, we suggest using a meat thermometer. Place it in the middle of the loaf before you place it in the oven. The meatloaf is done when the thermometer reads between 155 and 170 degrees Fahrenheit. After removing the loaf from the oven, let it sit for 10 to 15 minutes before slicing. This gives the loaf a chance to relax (nothing worse than a tense meatloaf) and keeps the juices from running out when you cut it. This rule applies to both meat and poultry loaves.

Serving. After the meatloaf has finished cooking, remove it from the oven and let it sit for 10 to 15 minutes. To remove the loaf to a serving platter, run a knife along the edges of the loaf to separate it from the pan.

Don't just dump the meatloaf onto a platter. It is liable to pop from the pan, bounce off the platter, and land on the floor . . . and vigilant dogs will devour it in seconds. We speak from experience. Instead, place the platter face down on top of the meatloaf pan. Using two potholders, grasp the plate and the meatloaf pan together, and turn it upside down. Carefully lift the pan from the loaf.

Wrapping it up. Cooked meatloaves freeze very well. If you want to freeze your meatloaf, wrap it in wax paper *and* aluminum foil. (We learned the hard way after spending a long afternoon picking frozen foil off a meatloaf.) Make sure the loaf is completely cooled before you freeze it.

To freeze an uncooked meatloaf, form the mixture into a loaf that will fit into a standard loaf pan (9 × 5 × 3 inches) or into a free-form loaf. For individual servings, divide the mixture into several portions and form miniloaves.

Wrap the uncooked loaf or loaves in wax paper and then in aluminum foil. Label the package so you know what it is and when you froze it. Remove the wax paper before cooking.

HOW TO TELL IF YOUR MEATLOAF IS DONE

Don't overcook your meatloaf. If your loaf is underdone, that's easy to remedy. But if you overcook it, you'll be left with a three-pound hockey puck.

The most accurate method for determining the doneness of meatloaf is to use a meat thermometer. Place the thermometer in the middle of the loaf *before* you place it in the oven. Or use an instant-read thermometer. The thermometer should read between 155 and 170 degrees Fahrenheit, depending on how well done you like your meat. Remember, meat continues to cook after it is removed from the oven, so time your cooking accordingly.

Don't slice the meatloaf at one end to see if it's cooked. All of the juices will run out, and you'll be left with a dry loaf. Instead, remove the loaf from the oven and quickly press it with your finger. If the meatloaf springs back to your touch, it should be done. Another sign that your loaf is done is if it pulls away from the sides of the pan.

Chapter 2

Meatloaves Just Like Mom Used to Make

*T*he recipes in this chapter do not require that you have previous cooking experience. Mom's recipes are all quick, and can usually be assembled in one mixing bowl. If you are a more experienced cook, you'll not only enjoy these easy-to-prepare recipes but appreciate the time you'll save.

The Grand Prize Winner of the 1992 Great American Meatloaf National Recipe Contest is in this chapter. Dianne C. Mahlert's Cape Cod Cranberry Meatloaf is on page 37, and shows that prize-winning recipes don't have to be complicated. As a matter of fact, Dianne's recipe can be put together in less than 10 minutes.

Sweet and Sour Meatloaf

•

JUDY KUSHNER-DeGROOT

HAMILTON, MASSACHUSETTS

WMHQ Note: To all of you single guys out there, this is a great loaf to make for that special someone. I tried it one night, and it had the desired effect: she didn't run out of the dining room clutching her throat. It's simple and easy to clean up. That's especially important if you do dishes as often as I do—the day after a total solar eclipse.

SERVES 6

Meatloaf

1½ pounds ground beef
½ teaspoon salt
½ teaspoon black pepper
1 cup tomato sauce
2 tablespoons prepared
  mustard

1 cup bread crumbs*
1 large egg, lightly beaten
1 small onion, minced

Sauce

1 cup tomato sauce
2 tablespoons distilled white
  vinegar

½ cup water
2 tablespoons light brown
  sugar, packed

*If necessary, add more bread crumbs a tablespoon at a time to make a firm loaf.

1. Preheat the oven to 350 degrees. Lightly oil a 10 × 13-inch roasting pan.

2. In a large bowl, mix all the meatloaf ingredients and shape into a loaf. Place the loaf into the prepared pan, leaving at least 1½ inches on all sides.

3. Mix all the sauce ingredients in a small bowl.

4. Pour the sauce over the top of the loaf and bake for 1¼ hours or until done. Baste the meatloaf as it cooks. Let the loaf sit for 10 minutes before serving.

Italian Meatloaf

●

GUY SAWDERS
LAS VEGAS, NEVADA

WMHQ Note: This basic loaf has the right blend of flavors. It proved pop-ular with our guests and our mascots (Tiffany, Scruffy, Penny, and Atticus).

Every organization needs mascots, and we have four of the best. Penny is my dog and was always there when something dropped toward the floor—and you could count on her to catch it before it landed. T. K.'s dogs, Scruffy and Tiffany, are better mannered. They'd wait until the food ac-tually landed before snarfing it up. Atticus, the cat, feigned disinterest in everything that was going on.

SERVES 6 to 8

1 pound lean ground beef
½ cup grated mozzarella cheese
6 ounces pepperoni, chopped
¼ teaspoon black pepper
40 saltine crackers, crushed*
1 6-ounce can tomato paste
1 to 2 tablespoons Italian seasoning†

1 medium white onion, finely chopped
1 tablespoon garlic powder
1 envelope (¾ ounce) mushroom gravy mix
2 large eggs, lightly beaten
5½ ounces beef broth

1. Preheat the oven to 375 degrees. Lightly oil a cookie sheet with sides.

2. In a large bowl, combine all the ingredients and mix well.

3. Form the meat mixture into a loaf and place it on the prepared cookie sheet.

4. Bake for 1½ hours or until done. Let the loaf sit for 10 minutes before serving.

*If necessary, add more cracker crumbs a tablespoon at a time to make a firm loaf.
†Guy's original recipe called for more Italian seasoning than the 2 tablespoons suggested above. Adjust to your taste.

Popeye Meatloaf

———————●———————

Doris B. Thomas
EASTON, CONNECTICUT

WMHQ Note: I hate spinach. I mean I really hate spinach, but this loaf has made me reconsider. I wish my mother had discovered this loaf 30 years ago.

SERVES 8 to 10

1 10-ounce package frozen
    spinach
3 pounds ground beef
1 pound Italian sausage,
    casing removed
½ cup plain bread crumbs*
½ cup freshly grated Parmesan
    or Romano cheese
1 tablespoon butter

2 tablespoons olive oil
1 cup diced onion
2 garlic cloves, minced
4 large eggs, lightly beaten
2 teaspoons Maggi†
⅛ teaspoon salt
⅛ teaspoon black pepper
2 strips bacon, uncooked

1. Preheat the oven to 350 degrees. Lightly oil a 10 × 13-inch roasting pan.

2. Thaw the frozen spinach and squeeze out the excess moisture. Coarsely chop the spinach leaves.

(continued)

*If necessary, add more bread crumbs a tablespoon at a time to make a firm loaf.
†Maggi, made by Nestlé, is a flavorful, organic seasoning agent that is usually found in the dry soup section of your supermarket. If you can't find Maggi, substitute 2 teaspoons of your favorite spice blend.

3. In a large bowl, place the ground beef, sausage, bread crumbs, grated cheese, and chopped spinach leaves. Mix and set aside.

4. In a skillet, melt the butter with the olive oil and sauté the onion and garlic until translucent, about 4 to 6 minutes. When cool, add the sautéed ingredients to the meatloaf mixture.

5. In a small bowl, combine the eggs, Maggi, salt, and pepper. Add this to the meat mixture. Mix well.

6. Shape the meat mixture into a loaf and place it in the prepared pan. Lay the bacon strips across the top of the meatloaf. Bake for 45 minutes to 1 hour, or until done.

Ralph's Egg-Cellent Meatloaf

RALPH GERKEN

CLEARWATER, FLORIDA

WMHQ Note: We didn't have a 12-inch glass baking dish. Instead, we used an iron skillet covered tightly with aluminum foil. This provides a steaming method and keeps the meatloaf moist. If you don't have the pan called for in a recipe, be creative. Just keep an eye on the loaf, since the cooking time will vary.

SERVES 8 to 10

Meatloaf

1 pound ground beef
1 pound ground veal
1 pound ground pork
2 teaspoons dry mustard
½ teaspoon garlic powder
¼ cup low-fat milk
1½ cups diced Spanish onions
½ cup chopped celery
¼ cup egg substitute

½ cup chopped fresh parsley
½ cup wheat germ
2 teaspoons Mrs. Dash
   seasoning mix
⅔ cup ketchup
1 cup Quaker Oats Plus Fiber
   or Multigrain cereal*
1 hard-boiled egg, peeled

Topping

⅓ cup ketchup

1. Preheat the oven to 350 degrees. Lightly oil a 12-inch square glass baking dish with cover.

2. In a large bowl, combine the ground beef, veal, and pork. Mix thoroughly.

3. Add the remaining ingredients to the meat mixture except the hard-boiled egg. Mix until all the ingredients are well combined.

4. Form the meat mixture into a loaf and set in the prepared pan. With your hands, form a well in the top of the loaf and insert the hard-boiled egg. Completely cover the egg with the meat mixture.

5. Bake for 1¼ hours with the cover on. Remove the cover, pour the ketchup over the meatloaf, and bake uncovered for an additional 15 minutes or until done. Let the loaf sit for 10 minutes before slicing.

*If necessary, add more cereal a tablespoon at a time to make a firm loaf.

Easy, Healthy, and Delicious Meatloaf

●

BARBARA ANN GAJDA
FALL RIVER, MASSACHUSETTS

WMHQ Note: Barbara took a basic meatloaf and made it healthier. The nonfat dry milk, low-fat milk, the egg substitute, and wheat germ make this a perfect loaf for people watching their cholesterol.

SERVES 4

1 pound lean ground beef
1 teaspoon onion powder
½ cup wheat germ
½ teaspoon garlic powder
¼ cup Italian flavored bread crumbs*
¾ teaspoon salt

3 tablespoons nonfat dry milk
¼ teaspoon black pepper
1 large egg, lightly beaten, or equivalent egg substitute
½ teaspoon poultry seasoning
¼ cup low-fat milk

1. Preheat the oven to 350 degrees. Lightly coat a 9 × 5 × 3-inch loaf pan with nonstick cooking spray.

2. In a large bowl, place all the ingredients and mix thoroughly.

3. Set the meat mixture into the prepared pan and bake for 1 hour or until done. Let the meatloaf sit for 10 minutes before slicing and serving.

*If necessary, add more bread crumbs a tablespoon at a time to make a firm loaf.

Vegetable Meatloaf

———————•———————

BETTY GIBBS
HANCEVILLE, ALABAMA

"This was the meatloaf I grew up on, and I never could figure out why meatloaf eaten in a restaurant tasted too dry. When I left home, my mother gave me this recipe. It was popular with my roommates and in later years I shared it with women who said their husbands wouldn't eat meatloaf. They liked this one. My husband is an onion lover so, since marrying him, I have increased the onion to at least 1 cup and sometimes add a dash of Worcestershire sauce."

—BETTY GIBBS

A Tip from Betty: If you're in a hurry, place the meatloaf mixture into individual muffin cups (fill about two-thirds full) and bake at 425 degrees for 20 minutes.

SERVES 6 to 8

2 pounds lean ground beef, or
   1 pound beef and 1 pound
   pork
2 large eggs, lightly beaten
½ cup chopped onion
¼ cup chopped green bell
   pepper

1 10¾-ounce can vegetable
   soup
2 cups Rice Krispies cereal*
⅛ teaspoon salt
⅛ teaspoon pepper

(*continued*)

*If necessary, add more cereal a tablespoon at a time to make a firm loaf.

1. Preheat the oven to 375 degrees. Lightly oil a 12 × 9 × 2-inch baking pan (or use a 9 × 13-inch baking dish).

2. In a large bowl, combine all the ingredients.

3. Form the meatloaf mixture into a loaf and set in the prepared pan. Bake for 1 hour or until done. (Drain the fat from the pan after 30 minutes of cooking.) Let the loaf sit for 10 minutes before slicing.

Tasty, Easy Meatloaf

———•———

GENEVIEVE PADYKULA

PAWTUCKET, RHODE ISLAND

WMHQ Note: Genevieve's meatloaf included two things we had not seen in a meatloaf recipe before: tapioca and baking powder. The result was a light and moist meatloaf.

SERVES 6

1 pound lean ground beef
½ pound ground pork
4 tablespoons instant tapioca
2 tablespoons Worcestershire
  sauce
½ teaspoon baking powder
1 tablespoon garlic powder
2 large eggs, lightly beaten

⅛ teaspoon salt
⅛ teaspoon black pepper
1 cup scalded milk*
1½ cups crushed saltine
  crackers†
1 medium onion, finely
  chopped

1. Preheat the oven to 325 degrees. Lightly oil a 9 × 5 × 3-inch loaf pan.

2. In a large bowl, combine the beef, pork, tapioca, Worcestershire sauce, baking powder, and garlic powder. Mix well.

3. To the mixture, add the eggs, salt, and black pepper and blend well.

4. Pour the scalded milk into a separate bowl, then add the crushed saltine crackers and onion. When the milk has been fully absorbed, add to the meat mixture.

5. Form the mixture into a loaf and place in the prepared pan. Bake for 1¼ hours or until done. Let the loaf sit for 10 minutes before slicing.

*Heat the milk (but do not boil) until small bubbles form around the edge.
†If necessary, add more cracker crumbs a tablespoon at a time to make a firm loaf.

Jimmy's Family's Favorite Meatloaf

————————————•————————————

JAMES HORODYSKI

KINSMAN, OHIO

WMHQ Note: This is a very quick loaf to assemble. We tried this recipe with the ground pork. If you want to omit the pork, add another ½ pound of ground beef to the recipe.

SERVES 6 to 8

Meatloaf

2 pounds ground beef
½ pound ground pork (optional)
2 large eggs, lightly beaten
½ cup milk
1 tablespoon steak sauce
½ teaspoon black pepper
¼ teaspoon garlic powder
½ teaspoon salt
¼ teaspoon onion powder

1 cup Italian-flavored bread crumbs*
1 medium–large onion, chopped
1 celery stalk, chopped
1 green bell pepper, chopped
1 4-ounce can mushrooms, drained and finely chopped

Topping

2 tablespoons ketchup

1. Preheat the oven to 350 degrees. Lightly oil an 8½-inch square pan with tight-fitting lid. (We used an iron skillet covered tightly with aluminum foil. This also provides a steaming method to keep the meatloaf moist.)

2. In a large bowl, combine all the ingredients and mix well.

3. Form the meat mixture into a loaf and place in the prepared pan.

4. Spread the ketchup over the top of the loaf. Cover and bake for 1½ hours or until done. Keep the lid on for the entire cooking time.

5. Drain all the grease after the first 45 minutes of baking and again before serving. Let the loaf sit for 10 minutes before slicing.

*If necessary, add more bread crumbs a tablespoon at a time to make a firm loaf.

Momma's Best Meatloaf

———————•———————

MARION JOHNSON
VIENNA, ILLINOIS

"This economical meatloaf recipe has been a favorite in my family for many years."
— MARION JOHNSON

WMHQ Note: This is the quintessential quick loaf. In fact, it takes longer to pronounce quintessential *than it takes to make it.*

SERVES 6

Sauce

4 tablespoons light brown
  sugar, packed
½ cup ketchup

2 tablespoons Worcestershire
  sauce
4 tablespoons distilled white
  vinegar

Meatloaf

1½ pounds lean ground beef
1 teaspoon salt
1 large egg, lightly beaten, or
  ¼ cup egg substitute
⅓ cup diced onion

¼ teaspoon black pepper
2 tablespoons ketchup
1 cup seasoned bread crumbs*
½ cup low-fat milk

(*continued*)

*If necessary, add more bread crumbs a tablespoon at a time to make a firm loaf.

1. Preheat the oven to 350 degrees. Lightly oil a 10-inch iron skillet.

2. To make the sauce, combine all the sauce ingredients in a saucepan and boil for 5 minutes.

3. In a large bowl, thoroughly mix all the meatloaf ingredients.

4. Set the meat mixture into the prepared skillet and shape the mixture into an oval loaf.

5. Pour the sauce over the loaf and bake for 1 hour or until done. Baste the meatloaf with the sauce occasionally while cooking.

6. Let the meatloaf cool 10 minutes before slicing.

The Meatloaf I Used to Hate

•

JILL PRICE
NEWINGTON, CONNECTICUT

"When I was about nine years old, I hated this meatloaf. I was sent to my room for refusing to eat it. Now, I love it, especially served cold on rye bread with a slice of onion and ketchup."

—JILL PRICE

WMHQ Note: This recipe uses matzo meal as the binder. A great idea!

SERVES 6

Meatloaf

1½ pounds ground beef
2 large eggs, lightly beaten
1 cup unsalted matzo meal*
1 large onion, chopped

¼ teaspoon salt
¼ teaspoon black pepper
¼ teaspoon parsley flakes
¼ teaspoon garlic powder

Topping

1 16-ounce can stewed tomatoes

1. Preheat the oven to 350 degrees. Lightly oil a 10 × 13-inch roasting pan.

2. In a large bowl, combine all the ingredients and mix well. Form the mixture into a rectangular shape and place in the prepared roasting pan.

3. Pour the stewed tomatoes over the meatloaf. Cover with aluminum foil and bake for 45 minutes.

4. Remove the foil and continue cooking for 30 minutes more or until done. Let the loaf sit for 10 minutes before serving.

*If necessary, add more matzo meal a tablespoon at a time to make a firm loaf.

Nancy's One-Pot Dinner Recipe

•

NANCY MILLETT

HAMDEN, CONNECTICUT

WMHQ Note: This recipe calls for an electric skillet. When we made this a second time, we did it in a regular skillet on the stove and it worked just as well. Make sure to add more water if the loaf starts to dry out. The great thing about this recipe is that the potatoes, vegetables, and meatloaf are all done at the same time. And there's only one pan to clean!

SERVES 6

3 tablespoons vegetable oil
1 small onion, chopped
1 large egg, lightly beaten
1 pound ground beef
¼ cup water
½ cup plain bread crumbs*

1 ½ teaspoons onion powder
1 ½ teaspoons garlic salt
4 medium potatoes, scrubbed
   and sliced
1 20-ounce bag frozen crinkle-
   cut carrots

1. Heat the oil in an electric skillet to 300 degrees. Turn the heat down to 250 degrees.

2. Place the onion in the bottom of the skillet.

*If necessary, add more bread crumbs a tablespoon at a time to make a firm loaf.

3. In a large bowl, mix the egg, beef, water, bread crumbs, onion powder, and garlic salt.

4. Shape the meat mixture in the bottom of the bowl to form a round loaf. Place the loaf in the skillet on top of the onion. Strew sliced potatoes around the meatloaf and the carrots on top of the potatoes. If desired, sprinkle the meatloaf and vegetables with extra onion powder and garlic salt.

5. Cover the skillet and cook for approximately 1 hour. About halfway through, turn the meatloaf over. (Using 2 spatulas helps when turning the meatloaf.) Stir the vegetables. To make sure everything is cooked, vegetables should be very tender and the meat should be a little crisp on the outside, staying juicy on the inside.

Easy This 'n That Meatloaf

───────●───────

ELAINE S. REIMAN
MARCO ISLAND, FLORIDA

WMHQ Note: This delicious loaf is a snap to put together. Because the recipe includes ground turkey, Elaine uses poultry seasoning, which adds a lot of flavor.

SERVES 6 to 8

Meatloaf

1 pound ground beef
1 pound ground turkey
1 cup crushed saltines or
   wheat crackers*
1 large egg, lightly beaten
1 medium onion, chopped

1 tablespoon parsley flakes
1 teaspoon poultry seasoning
1 tablespoon Worcestershire
   sauce
½ cup cubed cheddar cheese
⅛ teaspoon garlic powder

Topping

3 strips bacon, uncooked

½ cup tomato or V-8 juice

1. Preheat the oven to 350 degrees. Lightly oil a 9 × 5 × 3-inch loaf pan.

2. In a large bowl, mix all the ingredients. Press the meatloaf mixture into the prepared pan.

3. Place the bacon strips lengthwise on top of the loaf. Pour the tomato or V-8 juice over the loaf.

4. Bake for 1 hour or until done. Let the loaf sit for 10 minutes before serving.

*If necessary, add more cracker crumbs a tablespoon at a time to make a firm loaf.

**1991 FINALIST—THE GREAT AMERICAN MEATLOAF CONTEST,
NORTHEAST REGIONAL COOKOFF**

Meatloaf Manzella

JOSEPH MANZELLA
WESTON, CONNECTICUT

WMHQ Note: Peanut butter in a meatloaf? We were skeptical at first, too. Mr. Manzella's recipe created quite a stir at the 1991 contest. It was originally his mother's recipe, which he modified by adding peanut butter and walnuts. Not only does the peanut butter add flavor, but it gives the loaf a smooth texture.

SERVES 8 to 10

3 tablespoons butter
1 large onion, chopped
10 large scallions, chopped
1 medium carrot, finely chopped
5 celery stalks, chopped
1 red bell pepper, finely chopped
1 green bell pepper, finely chopped
4 garlic cloves, finely minced
⅛ teaspoon salt
1 teaspoon black pepper

¼ teaspoon cayenne pepper
½ teaspoon white pepper
1 teaspoon ground cumin
3 large eggs, lightly beaten
½ cup ketchup
½ cup half-and-half
1 cup chunky peanut butter
1 pound ground beef
1 pound ground veal
1 pound ground pork
1 cup chopped walnuts
1 small loaf French bread, crumbled*

(continued)

*If necessary, add more bread crumbs a tablespoon at a time to make a firm loaf.

1. Preheat the oven to 350 degrees. Lightly oil a 10-inch spring-form pan.

2. Heat the butter in a heavy skillet and add the onion, scallions, carrot, celery, red and green peppers, and garlic. Cook, stirring often, for about 10 minutes, or until all the moisture has evaporated. Remove from the heat and set aside to cool.

3. In a large mixing bowl, combine the salt, black pepper, cayenne, white pepper, cumin, and eggs. Beat well and add the ketchup, half-and-half, and peanut butter. Blend thoroughly.

4. Add the ground meats, walnuts, and bread crumbs to the mixture and blend thoroughly.

5. Add the cooled vegetables to the meat mixture and combine well.

6. Pack the mixture into the prepared pan and place inside a slightly larger baking pan. Pour boiling water into the larger pan about halfway up the side of the springform pan.

7. Bake for 1 hour or until done. Remove from the water and let the loaf stand 15 minutes before slicing.

Ground Beef with Bacon Meatloaf

———•———

JO-ANN R. LENTZ

HOLIDAY, FLORIDA

WMHQ Note: This meatloaf recipe tastes like stuffed green peppers. One of my father's favorite meals is stuffed peppers. He tried this loaf and loved it. Make sure you use a large green pepper or two small-to-medium ones.

S E R V E S 8 to 10

Meatloaf

2 tablespoons butter
1 large onion, diced
1 large green bell pepper, diced
3 pounds ground sirloin or lean ground beef
2 large eggs, lightly beaten
6 tablespoons steak sauce
5 tablespoons Kitchen Bouquet

3 tablespoons Worcestershire sauce
1 tablespoon coarsely ground black pepper
1½ tablespoons chopped fresh parsley
1 teaspoon celery seed
¼ cup bread crumbs*
8 strips thick-cut bacon, uncooked

Topping

1 teaspoon coarsely ground black pepper

(*continued*)

*If necessary, add more bread crumbs a tablespoon at a time to make a firm loaf.

1. Preheat the oven to 375 degrees. Lightly oil a 9 × 12 × 2-inch loaf pan.

2. In a large sauté pan, melt the butter over medium heat and add the onion and green pepper. Sauté for about 10 minutes or until the onion is translucent. Remove the pan from the heat and let the mixture cool.

3. In a large bowl, combine the ground sirloin, eggs, steak sauce, Kitchen Bouquet, Worcestershire sauce, black pepper, parsley, celery seed, and bread crumbs. Mix thoroughly.

4. Place the meat mixture into the prepared pan, leaving at least ¼ inch on all sides. Place the bacon strips on top of the loaf to cover completely. Sprinkle the top of the loaf with the 1 teaspoon of coarsely ground black pepper.

5. Bake for 45 minutes. Reduce the heat to 350 degrees and continue to cook for another 35 minutes or until done.

6. Let the loaf sit for 10 minutes. Using 2 spatulas, carefully remove the loaf from the pan and place on a serving platter.

Teddy's Best-Ever Moist Meatloaf

•

TEDDY LAMPE

NORTH RIDGE, CALIFORNIA

WMHQ Note: This loaf has the one ingredient that I love in any meatloaf: sausage. It adds a lot to the flavor. Substitute hot sausage if you prefer.

SERVES 8

Meatloaf

⅔ cup crushed cornflakes*
2 large eggs, lightly beaten
2 garlic cloves, crushed
1 small red onion, finely
  chopped
⅓ cup ketchup
2 tablespoons Worcestershire
  sauce
2 teaspoons seasoned salt

2 teaspoons black pepper
2 tablespoons sugar
¾ cup V-8 juice
2 cups milk
2 pounds ground sirloin or
  lean ground beef
¾ pound sweet Italian
  sausage, casing removed

Topping

⅓ cup hot ketchup†
1 tablespoon light brown
  sugar, packed

1 teaspoon onion powder
1 teaspoon garlic powder

(*continued*)

*If necessary, add more crushed cornflakes a tablespoon at a time to make a firm loaf.
†If you don't have hot ketchup, mix regular ketchup with a few drops of hot sauce.

1. Preheat the oven to 350 degrees. Lightly oil a 9 × 5 × 3-inch loaf pan.

2. In a large bowl, combine the cornflakes, eggs, garlic, red onion, ketchup, Worcestershire sauce, seasoned salt, black pepper, sugar, V-8 juice, and milk. Mix thoroughly.

3. In another bowl, mix the ground beef and sausage by hand. Add to the liquids in step 2. Thoroughly mix by hand, then place in the prepared loaf pan.

4. In a small bowl, combine the topping ingredients. Spread the topping over the meatloaf to cover.

5. Bake the meatloaf for 1 hour or until done. Remove the loaf from the oven, drain the fat. Let it sit for 15 minutes.

Cape Cod Cranberry Meatloaf

DIANNE C. MAHLERT
TALLAHASSEE, FLORIDA

"I was raised in the Midwest and 'comfort foods' like meatloaf are reminders of pleasant times. My husband, a New Englander, professed a dislike of meatloaf ('Dry and tasteless,' he said). So I set out to create a moist, flavorful loaf, and through the years, my Cape Cod Cranberry Meatloaf evolved. Depending on the season, I like to serve fresh vegetables with the dish—perhaps scalloped potatoes and crisp green beans in the winter, or new potatoes, corn on the cob, and thick tomato slices in the summer. With all meals, I like to pay attention to the colors on a plate.

"I am an avid cook and began this lifelong hobby when I received my first cookbook at the age of five. I now have over 200 cookbooks plus files of collected and created recipes." —DIANNE MAHLERT

WMHQ Note: This is a perfect combination of creativity and ease of preparation. At our meatloaf judging, this loaf came in first on all the ballots. It takes very little time to make, and the sauce is delicious! T. K., who is no big fan of cranberries, loved this loaf.

(*continued*)

SERVES 6

¾ cup whole cranberry sauce
¾ cup dark brown sugar,
   packed
1 pound ground beef
½ pound ground pork
1 pound ground veal
½ cup milk
1 medium onion, finely
   chopped

¼ cup ketchup
½ cup plain bread crumbs*
2 large eggs, lightly beaten
½ teaspoon dried thyme
½ teaspoon dried marjoram
¼ teaspoon white pepper
½ teaspoon dried rosemary
1 teaspoon salt
2 bay leaves

1. Preheat the oven to 350 degrees. Lightly oil a 9 × 5 × 3-inch loaf pan.

2. In a small bowl, combine the cranberry sauce and brown sugar.

3. Place the cranberry mixture in the bottom of the prepared loaf pan.

4. In a large bowl, combine the remaining ingredients except the bay leaves, and mix well.

5. Set the meatloaf mixture in the pan on top of the sauce.

6. Top the loaf with bay leaves and bake for 1¼ hours or until done.

7. Let the loaf cool 10 to 15 minutes. Remove the bay leaves. Carefully turn the loaf pan onto a serving platter. Drizzle pan juices, especially the cranberries, over the loaf before serving.

*If necessary, add more bread crumbs a tablespoon at a time to make a firm loaf.

Patty's Meatloaf

•

PATTY TRIPPEL
SOUTHBURY, CONNECTICUT

WMHQ Note: Evaporated milk does a great job of keeping a meatloaf moist and giving the meat a smoother texture. Patty's recipe is quick to prepare, and the combination of chili sauce and bacon for the topping is delicious.

SERVES 6

Meatloaf

1 5-ounce can evaporated milk
2 large eggs, lightly beaten
¾ cup crushed saltine
   crackers*
1½ pounds lean ground beef
1½ teaspoons salt
¼ teaspoon black pepper

1 teaspoon prepared mustard
1 teaspoon dry mustard
¾ cup chopped onion
4 strips bacon, cooked and
   crumbled
⅛ teaspoon crushed red
   pepper flakes

Topping

¾ cup chili sauce

3 strips bacon, uncooked

(continued)

*If necessary, add more cracker crumbs a tablespoon at a time to make a firm loaf.

1. Preheat the oven to 350 degrees. Lightly coat a 9 × 5 × 3-inch pan with nonstick cooking spray.

2. In a large bowl, combine all the meatloaf ingredients. Mix until well blended.

3. Press the meatloaf mixture into the prepared pan and then top the loaf with the chili sauce.

4. Lay the bacon on top and bake for 1 hour or until done. Let the loaf sit for 10 minutes before serving.

Tangy Stuffed Beef Loaf

ROBERT SCHERER

OCEAN CITY, NEW JERSEY

WMHQ Note: When you top a loaf (like this one) with bacon, you can reduce some of the fat by parboiling the bacon for a few minutes. Drop the bacon in boiling water, cook for 3 minutes, and then drain on a paper towel. You'll get rid of some of the fat, but retain the flavor.

SERVES 6

Meatloaf

1½ pounds ground beef
1 cup ketchup
1 cup plain bread crumbs or use Italian-flavored bread crumbs*
2 large eggs, lightly beaten
¼ cup parsley flakes
¼ cup chopped green bell pepper
1 tablespoon steak sauce

½ cup finely chopped onion
1 teaspoon garlic powder
½ teaspoon Worcestershire sauce
½ teaspoon salt
½ teaspoon black pepper
2 cups prepared packaged stuffing mix (such as Pepperidge Farm or Stove Top)

Topping

3 tablespoons ketchup

3 bacon strips, uncooked

1. Preheat the oven to 350 degrees. Lightly oil a shallow 9 × 13-inch baking dish.

2. In a large bowl, combine all the meatloaf ingredients except the stuffing. Mix well.

3. In the prepared baking dish, place half the meatloaf mixture. Make a shallow depression in the meatloaf. Prepare the stuffing mix according to package directions. Place the stuffing in the depression. Put the remaining meatloaf mixture over the stuffing and form into a solid loaf.

4. Spread the ketchup on top of the meatloaf. Arrange the bacon strips on top.

5. Bake for 1 hour or until done. Let it sit for 10 minutes before serving.

*If necessary, add more bread crumbs a tablespoon at a time to make a firm loaf.

Susan's Sweet-and-Sour Meatloaf

•

SUSAN M. BROWN

WEST HARTFORD, CONNECTICUT

WMHQ Note: Growing up across the street from the Browns, I knew Mrs. Brown was a good cook. This recipe is the proof. The sweet-and-sour sauce is delicious and can be used to top other meats as well.

SERVES 6

Meatloaf

1 large egg, lightly beaten
1 cup chili sauce
½ cup finely chopped onion
½ teaspoon salt

½ teaspoon black pepper
¾ cup rolled oats*
2 pounds ground beef

Topping

6 slices bacon, uncooked
5 ounces apple or guava jelly
1½ cups chili sauce

2 tablespoons fresh lemon
juice

*If necessary, add more oats a tablespoon at a time to make a firm loaf.

1. Preheat the oven to 350 degrees. Lightly oil a 7 × 11-inch glass baking dish.

2. In a large bowl, mix the egg, chili sauce, onion, salt, and pepper. Add the oats and ground beef. Mix thoroughly.

3. Shape into a loaf and place in the prepared baking dish.

4. Bake 45 minutes. While the loaf is baking, prepare the topping. Partly cook the bacon; do not let it get crisp. Drain the fat and set aside.

5. In a small saucepan, melt the jelly with the chili sauce. Mix well and remove from the heat. Add the lemon juice.

6. After 45 minutes, remove the loaf from the oven and drain off the accumulated fat. Arrange the bacon slices on top of the loaf.

7. Bake 15 minutes. Remove the loaf and drain the fat again. Pour ½ cup of the sauce over the loaf.

8. Bake another 15 minutes. Remove the loaf from the oven and cover with foil. Let it sit for 10 minutes. Run a sharp knife along the edges of the meatloaf. Use 2 spatulas to lift the loaf out of the pan and place on a serving platter. Warm the remaining sauce and serve it with the loaf.

Old-Fashioned Country Meatloaf

—•—

JUDITH HENBEST

ROCKFORD, ILLINOIS

WMHQ Note: Remember family picnics down by the stream right near the tree with the rope swing? Me neither, but this would be the perfect meatloaf for such an occasion.

SERVES 6 to 8

1½ pounds ground beef
½ pound ground pork
2 large eggs, lightly beaten
1 medium onion, finely minced
1 teaspoon salt
½ teaspoon black pepper
1 green bell pepper, finely chopped (optional)

¼ cup ketchup
2 tablespoons Worcestershire sauce
¼ cup milk
1½ cups old-fashioned rolled oats*
4 strips bacon, uncooked
1 8-ounce can tomato sauce

1. Preheat the oven to 350 degrees. Coat a 10-inch skillet with non-stick cooking spray.

2. In a large bowl, mix the ground beef and the ground pork.

3. Make a large well in the meat mixture. Into the well put the eggs, onion, salt, black pepper, green pepper, ketchup, Worcestershire sauce, milk, and oats. Mix thoroughly.

4. Form the meatloaf mixture into a loaf shape.

*If necessary, add more oats a tablespoon at a time to make a firm loaf.

5. Place 2 strips of the bacon crossed corner to corner in the bottom of the pan.

6. Place the loaf on the bacon and draw up the ends of the bacon onto the sides of the loaf. Cross the other 2 strips of the bacon on top of the loaf from alternate corners.

7. Bake for 1 hour. Pour the tomato sauce over the loaf and bake for an additional 30 minutes. Let the loaf sit for 15 minutes before slicing and serving.

Best-Ever Meatloaf

•

JEAN HORRIGAN SCOTT
MAUMEE, OHIO

WMHQ Note: We liked the idea of using Wheaties as a binder—it makes this the ''Meatloaf of Champions.'' This easy-to-prepare loaf is great in a sandwich the next day.

SERVES 4

Meatloaf

1 pound lean ground beef
1 cup Wheaties cereal*
1 cup tomato juice
1 large egg, lightly beaten

1 small onion, grated
  (approximately 2
  tablespoons)
½ teaspoon salt
⅛ teaspoon black pepper

Topping

¼ cup mild or hot salsa

1. Preheat the oven to 350 degrees. Lightly oil a 9 × 5 × 3-inch loaf pan.

2. In a large bowl, mix all the meatloaf ingredients.

3. Place the meatloaf mixture in the prepared pan.

4. Spread the salsa over the top of the meatloaf.

5. Bake uncovered for 1 hour or until done.

6. Let the meatloaf cool for 10 minutes. Run a sharp knife along the edges of the loaf to separate it from the pan. Lift the loaf out of the pan using 2 spatulas, so that the salsa remains on top.

*If necessary, add more cereal a little at a time to make a firm loaf.

German Applesauce Meatloaf Aunt Matilda

•

JOHN M. FRASE

NASHVILLE, TENNESSEE

"My Aunt Matilda made this meatloaf recipe, and when she did the whole family came to dinner (noon). She did not have the recipe written down and many years after her death, I cooked my way into the recipe as I have had to do with many of the old family recipes." —JOHN FRASE

WMHQ Note: This is one of my favorite meatloaves in the book. This loaf is simple to make and the applesauce adds terrific flavor and smooths the meat's texture. Served with homemade applesauce, it's a perfect winter dinner.

SERVES 6 to 8

1½ pounds ground beef
½ pound ground pork
½ cup finely diced onion
1 cup applesauce
1 large egg, lightly beaten

1 cup bread crumbs*
3 tablespoons ketchup
2 teaspoons salt
¼ teaspoon black pepper

1. Preheat the oven to 350 degrees. Lightly oil a 9 × 5 × 3-inch loaf pan.

2. In a large bowl, combine all the ingredients and mix well.

3. Place the meatloaf mixture in the prepared pan.

4. Bake for 1½ to 2 hours.

5. Let cool for 10 to 15 minutes. Turn the loaf out of the pan. Slice and serve.

*If necessary, add more bread crumbs a tablespoon at a time to make a firm loaf.

Meatloaf à la Sharin

———————— • ————————

SHARIN SLAVER

WEST ROXBURY, MASSACHUSETTS

*WMHQ Note: This is an ideal example of a "Just Like Mom Used to Make"
meatloaf. Serve this loaf with Italian bread to sop up the tomato sauce.*

SERVES 6 to 8

Meatloaf

1½ pounds ground beef
½ pound ground pork
1 medium onion, chopped
3 large eggs, lightly beaten
1 4-ounce can mushrooms,
   drained
½ cup plain bread crumbs*

2 teaspoons parsley flakes
1 teaspoon salt
½ teaspoon black pepper
1 14½-ounce can tomatoes
   with juice
1¼ cups shredded cheddar
   cheese

Optional Topping

1 tablespoon ketchup

1 tablespoon parsley flakes

1. Preheat the oven to 350 degrees. Lightly oil a 9 × 5 × 3-inch
loaf pan.

*If necessary, add more bread crumbs a tablespoon at a time to make a firm loaf.

2. In a large bowl, combine all the ingredients except the cheese, and mix well.

3. Place half the mixture in the prepared pan. Cover the mixture with the cheese and add the remaining meat mixture to the loaf pan.

4. If desired, add the ketchup and parsley flakes to the top of the loaf before baking.

5. Bake for 1½ hours or until done. Let the loaf sit for 10 minutes before slicing.

Baked Meatloaf Supreme

———————•———————

Josephine Devereaux Piro

EASTON, PENNSYLVANIA

WMHQ Note: This tastes just like the meatloaf my grandma makes. The secret of this loaf is using a little sugar. It helps bring out the rest of the flavors without making the loaf taste sweet.

S E R V E S 6 to 8

Meatloaf

3 strips bacon, uncooked
1 large egg
2 egg whites
½ cup skim milk
¼ teaspoon black pepper
¼ teaspoon dried thyme
1 cup Italian-flavored bread crumbs*

1 pound lean ground beef
½ pound lean ground veal
½ pound ground pork
½ cup chopped scallions (including green part)
2 tablespoons chopped fresh parsley
⅛ teaspoon garlic powder

Topping

⅛ teaspoon Dijon mustard
1 teaspoon sugar

⅓ cup chili sauce or ketchup

*If necessary, add more bread crumbs a tablespoon at a time to make a firm loaf.

1. Preheat the oven to 350 degrees. Lightly coat a piece of aluminum foil with nonstick cooking spray and line a 12 × 8 × 2-inch glass baking dish with the coated foil.

2. In a small skillet over medium heat, sauté the bacon until partly cooked but not brown. Drain on paper towels and set aside.

3. In a small bowl, lightly beat the whole egg, egg whites, milk, pepper, and thyme. Stir in the bread crumbs and let the mixture stand for 5 minutes.

4. In a large bowl, combine the ground beef, veal, pork, scallions, parsley, and garlic powder. Fold in the egg mixture until well blended.

5. Shape the meat mixture into a loaf approximately 10 × 4 inches. Arrange the bacon strips diagonally on top of the loaf. Bake for 45 minutes.

6. In a small bowl, combine the mustard, sugar and chili sauce or ketchup. Stir to blend. Remove the meatloaf from the oven. Brush the sauce over the meatloaf and return it to the oven. Bake 15 minutes longer or until done.

7. After removing the meatloaf from the oven, let it sit for 10 minutes before serving.

The Meatloaf of Experience

———————•———————

AGNES SANTMIRE, GLADYS FLOWERS, BESSIE RAMAGE, ALICE BOUTWELL, VERA MCKEE, MARCEIL GERDEMAN, FRANCES CLOUSER, MARY BRANDEBERRY, RUTH GARWOOD

BOWLING GREEN, OHIO

"Around a dining room table, nine residents of the Blakely Care Center in North Baltimore, Ohio, put their heads together and came up with the following recipe for the meatloaf contest. With 591 total years of cooking experience among them, they agreed on this recipe."   —CAROL JONES

"All the nine ladies who put their heads together to submit this recipe agreed upon the following guidelines for meatloaf:
1. It should be simple and easy to make.
2. The ingredients should not be expensive.
3. It should appeal to all members of the family."   —THE BLAKELY COOKS

SERVES 6 to 8

Meatloaf

1½ pounds ground beef
½ pound ground pork
½ cup ketchup
2 large eggs, lightly beaten
1½ teaspoons salt
½ teaspoon black pepper
1 cup diced stewed tomatoes
   with juice

¾ cup diced celery
½ cup diced onion
1 garlic clove, finely chopped
20 soda crackers, crushed*
¼ cup milk

*If necessary, add more crushed crackers a tablespoon at a time to make a firm loaf.

Topping

4 tablespoons ketchup

1. Preheat the oven to 350 degrees. Lightly oil a 9 × 5 × 3-inch loaf pan.

2. In a large bowl, combine the beef and pork. Add the remaining ingredients and mix well.

3. Place the meat mixture in the prepared pan.

4. Make a 1-inch-deep furrow down the middle of the meat mixture and fill with the ketchup.

5. Bake for 1 hour and 45 minutes or until done. Drain the grease, then let the loaf sit for 10 minutes before removing it to a platter.

The Great Meatloaf

———————•———————

STANLEY BEANS

BOULDER CITY, NEVADA

WMHQ Note: Stanley wasn't exaggerating when he named this very tasty loaf. Unlike some folks whose recipes include every spice on the shelf, this recipe is simple . . . and delicious.

SERVES 8

2 pounds ground beef
2 teaspoons Au Jus sauce mix*
½ teaspoon garlic powder
½ teaspoon salt
½ teaspoon black pepper
1 cup plain bread crumbs†

½ teaspoon celery seed
1 teaspoon parsley flakes
1 teaspoon Dijon mustard
1 cup taco sauce
2 large eggs, lightly beaten
½ cup grated Parmesan cheese

1. Preheat the oven to 350 degrees. Lightly oil a 9 × 5 × 3-inch loaf pan.

2. In a large bowl, mix the meat, sauce mix, garlic powder, salt, and pepper.

3. Add the rest of the dry ingredients, cheese, mustard, taco sauce, and eggs. Mix well and let rest in the refrigerator for up to 3 hours.

4. Set the meat mixture in the prepared pan. Bake for 1½ hours or until done. Let the loaf sit for 10 minutes before slicing.

---

*Au Jus sauce mix is usually available in the spice section of the foodstore. If unavailable, substitute 2 teaspoons Kitchen Bouquet or Gravy Master.
†If necessary, add more bread crumbs a tablespoon at a time to make a firm loaf.

Sweet Meatloaf

•———

PAM BOYLL

HOBART, INDIANA

"This recipe was given to me by a friend when I was talking about how much I disliked meatloaf. I have since handed it to other family members and friends. It is one of the most well-liked meals in my family. It is also great cold on sandwiches."   —PAM BOYLL

SERVES 4 to 6

Topping

1 cup ketchup
½ cup light brown sugar,
   packed

1 teaspoon dry mustard

Meatloaf

1 pound ground beef
½ pound ground pork
1 large egg, lightly beaten
¼ cup minced onion
3 tablespoons light brown
   sugar, packed
¼ teaspoon black pepper

¼ teaspoon dry mustard
¼ teaspoon dried sage
¼ teaspoon garlic salt
½ cup ketchup
3 slices bread, torn and soaked
   in 1 cup milk*

(*continued*)

*If necessary, add more soaked bread a tablespoon at a time to make a firm loaf.

1. Preheat the oven to 350 degrees. Lightly oil a 9 × 5 × 3-inch loaf pan.

2. In a small bowl, mix all the topping ingredients and set aside.

3. In a large bowl, mix all the meatloaf ingredients, adding the milk-soaked bread last.

4. Set the meatloaf mixture in the prepared pan. Bake for 45 minutes. Remove the loaf from the oven. Drain the grease and coat the loaf with the topping. Return the loaf to the oven for an additional 45 minutes or until done. Let the loaf sit for 10 minutes before slicing.

Nancy's No-Nonsense Blue-Collar Meatloaf

•

NANCY JO HILL
CERRITOS, CALIFORNIA

"This recipe is designed with a lower fat and sodium content. For years, I made meatloaf without these concerns, but when my husband developed high blood pressure, I wanted him still to be able to enjoy his favorite dish. That's when I went to light sour cream and reduced the sodium.... The secret ingredient for my meatloaf used to be a spice mix called lemon-herb garni. But, that was loaded with salt, so I switched to lemon pepper with no salt." —NANCY JO HILL

WMHQ Note: The lemon pepper is a wonderful seasoning agent. You might want to make a gravy and serve it with the loaf. Use drippings and mix them with some light sour cream and dash of, you guessed it—lemon pepper.

S E R V E S 8 to 10

3 pounds extra-lean ground
   beef
1 tablespoon low-sodium
   Worcestershire sauce
1 cup light sour cream

1 10¾-ounce can reduced-
   sodium tomato soup*
1 large egg, lightly beaten
1 teaspoon lemon pepper
1¼ cups plain bread crumbs†

1. Preheat the oven to 400 degrees. Lightly oil a 9 × 13-inch baking dish.

2. In a large bowl, combine all the ingredients except half the bread crumbs. Mix thoroughly.

3. Divide the meatloaf mixture into thirds. (Dividing the mixture into thirds will allow the meat to cook faster.) Form each third into a loaf. Roll each loaf in the remaining bread crumbs.

4. Place the loaves in the prepared baking dish.

5. Bake for 1 hour or until done. Let them sit for 10 minutes before serving.

*In a pinch, use a few tablespoons of ketchup and add an extra egg instead of the tomato soup.
†If necessary, add more bread crumbs a tablespoon at a time to make a firm loaf.

Cinnamon Raisin Toast Meatloaf

•

JAMES REDMOND

NEW YORK CITY

WMHQ Note: Using cinnamon raisin bread as a binder is a terrific idea! Toasting the bread is even better because it gives the consistency all meatloaves need.

SERVES 6

Meatloaf

1½ pounds ground beef
2 large eggs, lightly beaten
2 celery stalks, finely chopped
1½ cups seasoned bread
  crumbs*
3 pieces cinnamon raisin
  bread, toasted and crumbled

1¼ cups ketchup
2 tablespoons spicy brown
  mustard†
1 tablespoon garlic powder
1 tablespoon black pepper
2 slices Swiss cheese

Topping

2 slices Swiss cheese

1. Preheat the oven to 325 degrees. Lightly oil a 9 × 5 × 3-inch loaf pan.

---

*If necessary, add more bread crumbs a tablespoon at a time to make a firm loaf.
†James recommends using a lot more spicy brown mustard than is listed above. It's up to you.

2. In a large bowl, combine all the meat mixture ingredients. Mix well.

3. Place the meatloaf mixture in the prepared pan. Bake for 1 hour, or until well done. Remove the loaf and lay topping cheese slices over the loaf. Return the loaf to the oven until the cheese browns. Let it sit for 10 minutes before slicing.

Mama's Magical Meatloaf

•

NAOMI FRISING
SHRUBOAK, NEW YORK

"My daughter Susan encouraged me to enter my creation in the contest. It's a family favorite."

SERVES 6

1 pound ground beef
½ pound ground pork
2 garlic cloves, chopped
2 large eggs, lightly beaten
¼ cup chopped fresh parsley
⅛ cup plus 1 tablespoon
    chopped fresh oregano
1 small onion, finely chopped
2 small ripe tomatoes, peeled

1 14½-ounce can stewed
    tomatoes
1 8-ounce can tomato sauce*
⅛ teaspoon salt
⅛ teaspoon black pepper
⅛ teaspoon dried basil
1½ cups Pepperidge Farm
    Herb Stuffing mix†

(*continued*)

---

*Naomi recommends using Sauce Arturo gourmet tomato sauce.
†If necessary, add more stuffing mix a tablespoon at a time to make a firm loaf.

1. Preheat the oven to 350 degrees. Lightly oil a 10 × 13-inch roasting pan.

2. In a large bowl, combine the meat, garlic, eggs, parsley, oregano, and onion.

3. Mix in the tomatoes and tomato sauce. Add the salt, pepper, basil, and stuffing mix. Mix well.

4. Shape the meatloaf mixture in the form of a football and place in the prepared pan. Cook for 1 hour or until done. Let it sit 10 minutes before slicing.

Barbara's Meatloaf

BARBARA LANE
PINEHURST, NORTH CAROLINA

WMHQ Note: This moist meatloaf has a great texture—wheat germ, oats, wheat bread, and turkey are tasty, healthy additions. We recommend (especially for this loaf) using an aluminum pan with slits cut in the bottom that allows the bacon to drip out onto a foil-lined pan.

SERVES 4 to 6

Meatloaf

1 pound ground beef
½ pound ground turkey
1 large onion, chopped
1 teaspoon salt
½ teaspoon black pepper
2 large eggs, lightly beaten
1½ cups crushed cornflakes

1½ cups rolled oats*
6 slices wheat bread, shredded
¾ cup wheat germ
3 tablespoons Worcestershire sauce
1 cup milk
12 saltine crackers, crushed

Topping

2 slices bacon, uncooked

3 tablespoons ketchup

1. Preheat the oven to 350 degrees. Lightly oil a 9 × 5 × 3-inch loaf pan.

2. In a large bowl, combine the meatloaf ingredients thoroughly.

3. Place the bacon in the bottom of the prepared pan. Set the meatloaf mixture on top of the bacon.

4. Spread the loaf with the ketchup and bake for 1 hour or until done. Let the loaf sit for 10 minutes before serving.

*If necessary, add more oats a tablespoon at a time to make a firm loaf.

Rich's Cheesy Meatloaf

———•———

RICHARD HOWARD
CROMWELL, CONNECTICUT

"An old girlfriend gave me the basic recipe around 1975. The soup replaced the tomato sauce shortly thereafter at a friend's suggestion. The dry mustard was added a year or so later at another friend's suggestion. The cheese, celery, and basil were my own ideas. It tastes good with or without ketchup."

—RICHARD HOWARD

WMHQ Note: Velveeta worked great in this loaf. I'm an avowed Velveeta-aholic. This loaf was a huge hit with my Wednesday night poker friends.

SERVES 4 to 6

1¼ pounds ground beef
1 cup seasoned bread crumbs*
⅔ 10¾-ounce can tomato soup
1 large egg, lightly beaten
1 medium onion, chopped
⅓ cup chopped celery

¼ cup chopped fresh parsley
¾ cup cubed Velveeta cheese
1 tablespoon dry mustard
1 tablespoon dried basil
1 teaspoon black pepper
1 teaspoon garlic powder

1. Preheat the oven to 350 degrees. Lightly oil a 9 × 5 × 3-inch loaf pan.

2. In a large bowl, combine all the ingredients and mix thoroughly.

3. Place the meatloaf mixture in the prepared pan and bake for 1 hour or until done. Let it sit for 10 minutes before slicing.

*If necessary, add more bread crumbs a tablespoon at a time to make a firm loaf.

The Silva Plate Special

———————●———————

GINNY SILVA

EVERETT, MASSACHUSETTS

WMHQ Note: We love Grape-Nuts. We love meatloaf. We love Grape-Nuts in meatloaf. Like other cereals, Grape-Nuts is an excellent binder.

SERVES 6

Meatloaf

2 pounds lean ground beef
¾ cup Grape-Nuts cereal
2 cups Italian-flavored bread
   crumbs*
2 large eggs, lightly beaten
1 tablespoon chopped fresh
   parsley
½ medium onion, grated

2 tablespoons sweet relish
2 medium carrots, grated
1 4-ounce can tomato sauce
½ green bell pepper, grated
⅛ teaspoon garlic powder
3 tablespoons chopped
   pimiento
⅛ teaspoon salt

Topping

½ cup tomato sauce

4 strips bacon, uncooked

1. Preheat the oven to 375 degrees. Lightly oil a 9 × 5 × 3-inch loaf pan.

2. In a large bowl, combine all the meatloaf ingredients and mix well. Place the meat mixture in the prepared pan.

(continued)

---

*If necessary, add more bread crumbs a tablespoon at a time to make a firm loaf.

3. Spread the tomato sauce on the loaf and place the bacon on top.

4. Bake for 1 hour or until done. Let the loaf sit for 10 minutes before slicing. (Ginny recommends removing the loaf to an *unwaxed* paper plate to absorb the grease.)

Ketchup Lovers' Meatloaf

STEPHANIE DREHS

LOCKPORT, NEW YORK

WMHQ Note: This is a real "Just Like Mom Used to Make" loaf. The seasonings are well proportioned without being overpowering.

SERVES 6

Meatloaf

1 garlic clove, minced
1 small onion, minced
1 tablespoon olive oil
1½ pounds ground beef
¾ cup Italian-flavored bread
  crumbs*

¼ cup grated Romano cheese
½ teaspoon salt
½ teaspoon black pepper
1 tablespoon parsley flakes
1½ teaspoons dried basil
1 large egg, lightly beaten

*If necessary, add more bread crumbs a tablespoon at a time to make a firm loaf.

Topping

1 cup ketchup

1. Preheat the oven to 350 degrees. Lightly oil a 9 × 13-inch baking pan.

2. In a medium skillet, sauté the garlic and onion in olive oil until the onion is translucent, about 4 to 6 minutes. Set aside to cool.

3. In a large bowl, combine the meat, bread crumbs, cheese, salt, black pepper, parsley, basil, sautéed onion and garlic, and egg. Mix well.

4. Form the mixture into a loaf and place in the prepared pan.

5. Bake for 1 hour. Spread ketchup over the outside of the loaf. Return the loaf to the oven for 10 to 15 minutes or until done. Let the loaf sit for 10 minutes before serving.

Bert's Meatloaf

•

BERT GOTTLIEB

SADDLE RIVER, NEW JERSEY

WMHQ Note: Bert. Sausage. Spices. Poker Game. Perfect.

SERVES 6 to 8

2 tablespoons butter
¾ cup finely chopped onion
¾ cup finely chopped scallions
¼ cup finely chopped celery
¼ cup finely chopped green
  bell pepper
¼ cup finely chopped red bell
  pepper
2 garlic cloves, minced
2 large eggs, lightly beaten
½ cup half-and-half

⅛ teaspoon cayenne pepper
½ teaspoon white pepper
1 teaspoon ground cumin
½ teaspoon grated nutmeg, or
  ⅛ teaspoon ground allspice
⅛ teaspoon salt
½ cup ketchup
2 pounds ground beef
¾ pound bulk sausage
½ cup bread crumbs*

1. Preheat the oven to 375 degrees. Lightly oil a 9 × 5 × 3-inch loaf pan.
2. Melt the butter in a large skillet and sauté the onion, scallions, celery, peppers, and garlic for 5 minutes. Remove to a small bowl and allow to cool.
3. In a large bowl, combine the eggs and half-and-half. Add the cayenne, white pepper, cumin, nutmeg or allspice, salt, and ketchup.
4. Add the meat and bread crumbs. Mix well.
5. Place the meatloaf mixture in the prepared pan. Place the loaf pan in a larger pan filled with water; the water should reach halfway up the sides of the pan. Cook for 1¼ hours or until done. Let stand for 10 minutes before slicing.

*If necessary, add more bread crumbs a tablespoon at a time to make a firm loaf.

Chapter 3

Meatloaves Like Mom Used to Make— with a Twist

What's the twist? Each of these recipes does something a little different to dress up a basic meatloaf.

Included in this section are some of the finalists from the 1991 Great American Meatloaf Contest. Anne Frederick's Spiced Lamb Loaf (page 90) has a delicious cheese sauce, which also can be used over vegetables. If you like Oriental spices and seasonings, try Deborah Puette's Tangy Oriental Meatloaf (page 78).

There are many sauces in the following recipes that stand on their own. They can be used with other meats, on vegetables, and on pasta.

The fillings that are featured in Margaret Wilson's Four M Meatloaf (page 84) or the stuffed meatloaf created by Shirley Perkiss (page 74) provide an easy way to combine many different flavors in one loaf.

Apple-Thyme Meatloaf

———————•———————

MIL KLEIN

FOUNTAIN VALLEY, CALIFORNIA

WMHQ Note: Apples, cooked ham, brown sugar, and dried thyme combine to make this a fantastic meatloaf. Because the ham has salt, I wouldn't recommend adding salt to the dish.

SERVES 6 to 8

Topping

4 medium Pippin apples,
  peeled, cored, and cut into
  ½-inch slices
¾ cup light brown sugar,
  packed

1 tablespoon water
1 teaspoon dried thyme
Thyme sprigs for garnish
  (optional)

Meatloaf

1½ pounds lean ground beef
1 pound ground cooked ham
1 cup applesauce
1 cup crumbled French bread*

¾ cup chopped onion
1 large egg, lightly beaten
2 tablespoons dry sherry
1 teaspoon dried thyme

*If necessary, add more bread crumbs a tablespoon at a time to make a firm loaf.

1. Preheat the oven to 350 degrees. Lightly coat a 9 × 13-inch baking dish with nonstick cooking spray.

2. In a small bowl, stir together the brown sugar, water, and 1 teaspoon thyme for the topping. Set aside.

3. In a large bowl, combine the ground beef, ham, applesauce, bread crumbs, onion, egg, sherry, and thyme. Mix thoroughly.

4. Shape into a 9 × 5-inch loaf and place in the prepared pan.

5. Bake the loaf for 30 minutes. Remove the loaf from the oven and arrange the apple slices around the meatloaf. Drizzle the topping over the apples.

6. Continue cooking an additional 30 minutes or until done, basting occasionally with the glaze. Let the loaf sit for 10 minutes before slicing.

1991 FINALIST—THE GREAT AMERICAN MEATLOAF CONTEST, NORTHEAST REGIONAL COOKOFF

Carole's Yogurt Meatloaf

CAROLE ROBERTS

PORT JEFFERSON, NEW YORK

WMHQ Note: Carole devised this Greek-inspired recipe and the judges loved it. She uses rye bread and wheat bread as binders in this recipe. Experiment with different types of bread and you'll be surprised what a difference in taste and texture it makes.

SERVES 6 to 8

Meatloaf

6 tablespoons chopped green bell pepper
¼ teaspoon chopped garlic
3 tablespoons chopped shallots
3 tablespoons chopped red onion
2 tablespoons olive oil
1 slice rye bread*
3 slices wheat bread*
¼ cup Madeira wine

1 pound lean ground beef
1½ pounds ground sirloin
1 teaspoon salt
2 large eggs, lightly beaten
½ cup grated Parmesan cheese
¾ cup plain yogurt
¼ cup prepared horseradish
1 teaspoon dried dill
½ cup sour cream
½ cup milk

*If necessary, add more bread a tablespoon at a time to make a firm loaf.

Topping

1 teaspoon chili powder

¼ cup Madeira wine
(optional)

Yogurt Sauce

1 cup plain yogurt
½ teaspoon dried dill

3 tablespoons chopped red
onion

1. Preheat the oven to 350 degrees. Lightly oil an 11 × 7½ × 3½-inch baking pan.

2. In a medium skillet, sauté the green pepper, garlic, shallots, and red onion in olive oil until soft. Set aside to cool.

3. In a large bowl, place the rye bread and wheat bread. Pour the wine over the bread and let soak until all the moisture is absorbed.

4. Mash the bread with a fork. Add the beef, sautéed vegetables, salt, eggs, and Parmesan cheese.

5. In a small bowl, mix the yogurt, horseradish, dill, sour cream, and milk. Stir thoroughly and add to the meat mixture. Mix well and place the mixture in the prepared pan.

6. Bake for 30 minutes. Add the wine and chili powder to the top of the meatloaf and continue cooking for 30 minutes or until done. Let the loaf sit for 10 minutes before slicing.

7. In a small bowl, combine the yogurt sauce ingredients, and serve with the meatloaf.

Apple Harvest Meatloaf

— • —

MARCI JAMES
TOLLAND, CONNECTICUT

WMHQ Note: For the apple lovers in the crowd, this is the meatloaf for you! Marci uses a combination of fresh apples, applesauce, apple juice, and nutmeg.

SERVES 6 to 8

Meatloaf

2 large eggs
1 teaspoon salt
¼ teaspoon black pepper
1½ teaspoons dried thyme
1 teaspoon grated nutmeg
½ teaspoon ground cloves
1½ pounds lean ground beef
½ pound ground pork
¾ cup crushed whole wheat
  Ritz crackers

1½ cups quick oats*
½ cup applesauce
½ cup apple cider or apple
  juice
¼ cup ketchup
½ cup finely diced onion
¼ cup finely diced celery
2 apples, peeled and thinly
  sliced (Cortland, Empire, or
  Granny Smith, if possible)

Topping

½ cup ketchup

½ cup light brown sugar,
  packed

*If necessary, add more oats a tablespoon at a time to make a firm loaf.

1. Preheat the oven to 350 degrees. Lightly oil a 10 × 10 × 2-inch baking dish. If desired, two 9 × 5 × 3-inch loaf pans may be used instead of the large square pan.

2. In a small bowl, beat the eggs with a whisk or rotary beater. Add the salt, pepper, thyme, nutmeg, and cloves. Mix well.

3. In a large bowl, combine the ground beef and ground pork. Stir in the egg mixture, then add the crushed crackers and oats.

4. Stir into the meatloaf mixture the applesauce and cider or juice. Add the ketchup and stir. Combine the diced onion and celery with the meatloaf mixture.

5. Place one-third of the meatloaf mixture in the bottom of the prepared pan. Add a layer of apples. Add a second layer of the meat mixture and then another layer of apples. Finish with a layer of the meatloaf mixture.

6. Bake for 50 minutes.

7. While the meatloaf is cooking, combine the brown sugar and ketchup in a small bowl. After the meatloaf has cooked for 50 minutes, remove from the oven and spread the topping over the meatloaf.

8. Continue baking for 10 minutes or until done. Remove from the oven and drain the excess fat. Let it sit for 10 minutes before slicing.

My Original Recipe for Stuffed Meatloaf

SHIRLEY F. PERKISS

SEAL BEACH, CALIFORNIA

WMHQ Note: The homemade stuffing is in the meatloaf! The stuffing stands on its own and would be perfect to serve with other dishes as well.

SERVES 6

Meatloaf

1¾ pounds lean ground beef
1 large egg, lightly beaten
1 tablespoon garlic powder
½ cup plain bread crumbs*
1 tablespoon chili powder

1 teaspoon salt
1 medium onion, finely
   chopped
½ teaspoon black pepper

Stuffing

1½ cups plain bread crumbs
1 large egg, lightly beaten
½ cup finely chopped celery
1 small onion, chopped
1 tablespoon flour

½ teaspoon salt
2 small garlic cloves, finely
   chopped, or 1 teaspoon
   garlic powder
½ teaspoon black pepper

*If necessary, add more bread crumbs a tablespoon at a time to make a firm loaf.

Topping

½ cup ketchup

1. Preheat the oven to 350 degrees. Lightly oil a 9 × 5 × 3-inch loaf pan.

2. In a large bowl, mix all the meatloaf ingredients until well blended. Place half the meat mixture in the prepared pan.

3. In another large bowl, mix all the stuffing ingredients until well blended. Place the stuffing mixture evenly over the meat mixture and set in the pan.

4. Place the remainder of the meat mixture evenly over the stuffing.

5. Pour the ketchup over the meatloaf.

6. Bake for 1 hour or until done. Turn off the oven and let the meatloaf stand in the warmed oven for 10 to 15 minutes or until set. Slice and serve.

Spirited Loaf

•

KRISTEN FRIZ

ALBURTIS, PENNSYLVANIA

WMHQ Note: Kristen and her mother, Rita Lawrence, made the long trip from Alburtis, Pennsylvania (near Allentown), to Hartford for the cookoff. The sauce she created for this loaf is sensational!

SERVES 8 to 10

Meatloaf

1 large onion, chopped
3 tablespoons butter
1½ cups half-and-half
1 cup crushed saltine crackers*
4 teaspoons Worcestershire sauce
½ teaspoon grated nutmeg

¼ teaspoon hot sauce
1 teaspoon salt
2 teaspoons garlic powder
½ teaspoon ground ginger
¼ teaspoon black pepper
4 pounds lean ground beef

*If necessary, add more cracker crumbs a tablespoon at a time to make a firm loaf.

Spirited Sauce

1 cup brandy
1 teaspoon vermouth
1 16-ounce jar peach preserves

¾ cup light brown sugar,
  packed
¼ teaspoon grated nutmeg

1. Preheat the oven to 400 degrees. Coat a 10-inch Bundt pan with butter-flavored cooking spray.

2. In a small skillet, sauté the onion in butter until translucent, about 4 to 6 minutes. Set aside and cool.

3. In a large bowl, combine the sautéed onion, half-and-half, cracker crumbs, Worcestershire sauce, and seasonings. Add the meat to the mixture and mix thoroughly.

4. Press the meatloaf mixture into the prepared pan. Bake for 45 minutes. Take the pan from the oven and, with a turkey baster, remove the grease and reserve 3 tablespoons of the drippings. Continue baking for 45 more minutes or until done. (Cover with aluminum foil if the top of the loaf is browning too quickly.)

5. Meanwhile, place the 3 tablespoons of meatloaf drippings in a medium saucepan and add the sauce ingredients. Simmer on low heat for 5 minutes.

6. Remove the meatloaf from the oven and let it cool for 15 minutes before unmolding. Unmold onto a serving platter and drizzle the sauce over the meatloaf right before serving.

Tangy Oriental Meatloaf

———————•———————

DEBORAH PUETTE
LILBURN, GEORGIA

"My family absolutely loves Oriental food. I tried to find just the right combination of flavors. I think I have succeeded."   —DEBORAH PUETTE

WMHQ Note: *This is a great combination of flavors. If you haven't tried hoisin sauce, taste it first before slathering it on the loaf. Or serve the sauce on the side. A little goes a long way!*

SERVES 6 to 8

Meatloaf

1 tablespoon peanut oil
½ cup finely chopped onion
2 garlic cloves, minced
1 teaspoon minced fresh ginger

2 pounds lean ground beef
¼ cup soy sauce
3 tablespoons sugar
1½ cups fresh bread crumbs*

Sauce

1 cup jellied cranberry sauce
¼ cup hoisin sauce

¼ cup honey

*If necessary, add more bread crumbs a tablespoon at a time to make a firm loaf.

1. Preheat the oven to 350 degrees. Lightly coat a 9 × 5 × 3-inch loaf pan with nonstick cooking spray.

2. In a small skillet, heat the oil over low heat. Add the onion, garlic, and ginger. Sauté for 3 to 4 minutes or until the onion is tender.

3. In a large mixing bowl, mix the sautéed ingredients, beef, soy sauce, sugar, and bread crumbs.

4. Press the mixture into the prepared pan. Bake for 1 hour or until done.

5. Meanwhile, in a small saucepan over low heat, mix the sauce ingredients and cook until the cranberry sauce is dissolved.

6. Drain the meatloaf. Pour the sauce over the meatloaf and return it to the oven and cook for 20 minutes. Let the meatloaf sit for 10 minutes before slicing.

Heart Smart Pilgrim Meatloaf

●

LISA KEYS

MIDDLEBURY, CONNECTICUT

WMHQ Note: Pumpkins and cranberries dress up a tasty Halloween-time loaf. Pumpkin lovers will want to use the Spicy Pumpkin Ketchup year-round as a topping for burgers and other meats.

SERVES 6

Spicy Pumpkin Ketchup

1½ cups canned pumpkin
1 medium onion, finely
  chopped
½ cup cider vinegar
½ cup applesauce
¼ teaspoon ground cloves

¼ teaspoon ground allspice
¼ teaspoon cayenne pepper
¼ teaspoon black pepper
4 tablespoons light brown
  sugar, packed
½ teaspoon curry powder
1 cup water

Meatloaf

1¼ pounds extra-lean ground
  beef
¾ cup rolled oats*

⅓ cup chopped onion
½ cup skim milk
1 egg white

*If necessary, add more oats a tablespoon at a time to make a firm loaf.

Optional Garnish

Boston lettuce leaves   Whole fresh cranberries

1. Preheat the oven to 350 degrees. Lightly oil a 9 × 5 × 3-inch loaf pan.

2. Combine the ingredients for ketchup in a medium saucepan. Simmer over medium-low heat for 1 hour. Measure out ½ cup for recipe and place the remainder in the refrigerator.

3. In a large bowl, combine all the ingredients for meatloaf, including ½ cup Spicy Pumpkin Ketchup. Blend well.

4. Press the meat mixture into the prepared pan.

5. Bake the meatloaf for 1 hour or until done; drain any excess grease. Let the loaf sit for 10 minutes. Remove the meatloaf to a lettuce-lined platter. Garnish with cranberries. Serve with Spicy Pumpkin Ketchup.

1991 FINALIST—THE GREAT AMERICAN MEATLOAF CONTEST, NORTHEAST REGIONAL COOKOFF

The Good Loaf

SISSY WILLIS

CHELSEA, MASSACHUSETTS

WMHQ Note: Sissy did something unusual in this recipe. She shaped the loaf like a cat and used some of the extra mixture to make a small mouse. If you'd like to try it, the instructions are noted at the bottom of the recipe. If you don't want to shape it like a cat, use a 9 × 5 × 3-inch loaf pan. This is a well-seasoned loaf. Try it and see why the judges liked it so much!

SERVES 6 to 8

Fruit Mixture

1 apple, cored, peeled, and
 coarsely chopped
½ pear, cored, peeled, and
 coarsely chopped

½ banana, sliced
4 strawberries (fresh or frozen)

Meatloaf

1 medium onion
6 garlic cloves
2 sprigs fresh oregano*
2 sprigs fresh thyme*
2 sprigs fresh marjoram*
2 sprigs fresh parsley*
1 cup fresh bread crumbs†
2 tablespoons Dijon mustard

1 teaspoon Worcestershire
　sauce
¼ cup apple cider
¼ cup tomato juice
1½ pounds lean ground beef

Additional Ingredients for Cat
4 raisins
Leafless parsley stems

1. Preheat the oven to 350 degrees. Lightly oil a 10 × 13-inch roasting pan.

2. In a small bowl, combine the fruit mixture.

3. Mince the onion, garlic, and herbs in a food processor or by hand with a sharp knife. Add to the fruit mixture. Place the mixture in a medium saucepan and warm over low heat, stirring frequently, until the fruit is soft, but not mushy, about 4 minutes.

4. Pour the mixture into a large bowl. Add bread crumbs, mustard, Worcestershire sauce, cider, and tomato juice. Mix thoroughly. Add the ground beef and mix until all the ingredients are incorporated.

5. If making a simple loaf, shape into an oval loaf. Bake 45 minutes to 1 hour, or until done.

If making into a cat, place the meatloaf mixture on a foil-lined baking dish. Shape into an oval loaf roughly the size of a cat and use the side of your hand to make an indentation for a tail along one side. Use your thumb and index finger to pinch up triangles for the ears at the other end. Shape the muzzle, add the raisins for the eyes, and insert parsley stems for whiskers. Kids will love this.

---

*If using fresh herbs, remove and retain leaves only. If you don't have fresh herbs, use 1 teaspoon dried.
†If necessary, add more bread crumbs a tablespoon at a time to make a firm loaf.

Four M Meatloaf (Margaret's Mushroom Muenster Meatloaf)

MARGARET WILSON
NEW BRITAIN, CONNECTICUT

WMHQ Note: Margaret's Muenster and mushroom melange makes much of a mild-mannered meatloaf. Mangia!

SERVES 6

Meatloaf

1 large egg, lightly beaten
¼ cup water
½ cup ketchup
1 envelope (0.9 ounce) Lipton
   Onion/Mushroom Soup mix

2 pounds ground sirloin
1 slice bread, crumbled*
½ cup rolled oats

Filling

1 cup chopped fresh
   mushrooms
2 tablespoons margarine
10 to 12 fresh basil leaves,
   chopped

¼ teaspoon dried oregano
4 ounces Muenster cheese,
   sliced

*If necessary, add more bread crumbs a tablespoon at a time to make a firm loaf.

1. Preheat the oven to 350 degrees. Lightly oil a 9 × 5 × 3-inch loaf pan.

2. In a large bowl, combine the egg, water, ketchup, and soup mix.

3. Add the ground beef, fresh bread crumbs, and oats, mixing well.

4. Place half the meat mixture into the bottom of the prepared pan.

5. Sauté the mushrooms in the margarine.

6. Place a layer of the sautéed mushrooms on top of the meatloaf. Layer the basil leaves, oregano, and then Muenster cheese on top of the mushrooms.

7. Place the remaining meat mixture on top of the layered filling.

8. Bake for 1¼ hours or until done. Let the loaf sit for 10 minutes before slicing.

Empress Meatloaf with Mushroom Stuffing

ALBINA MATUSHAK

MANCHESTER, CONNECTICUT

WMHQ Note: Albina's recipe includes fresh bread crumbs and they really make a difference in the texture. When we make a loaf calling for fresh bread crumbs, we either leave the bread out overnight, or toast fresh slices of bread until they're lightly brown, then crumble them.

SERVES 6 to 8

2 3-ounce cans sliced
   mushrooms, liquid reserved
½ cup minced onion
4 tablespoons butter
4 cups fresh bread crumbs*
¼ teaspoon dried thyme
¼ cup minced fresh parsley

2½ pounds ground beef
2 large eggs, lightly beaten
1½ teaspoons salt
⅛ teaspoon black pepper
⅓ cup ketchup

1. Preheat the oven to 375 degrees. Lightly oil a 9 × 5 × 3-inch loaf pan.

2. Sauté the mushrooms and onion in the butter until the onion is translucent, about 4 to 6 minutes.

3. In a small bowl, combine the sautéed mushrooms and onion with the bread crumbs, thyme, and parsley.

*If necessary, add more bread crumbs a tablespoon at a time to make a firm loaf.

4. In a large bowl, mix the beef, eggs, salt, black pepper, ketchup, and reserved mushroom liquid.

5. Pack half the meat mixture into the prepared pan. Place the mushroom stuffing on top, then cover with the remaining meat mixture.

6. Bake for 1¼ hours or until done.

7. Let the meatloaf sit for 15 minutes before serving. Drain the juices and turn out onto a serving plate.

Pizza Meatloaf

———————•———————

ELEANOR H. GABRIEL

LAS VEGAS, NEVADA

WMHQ Note: Eleanor took the basic pizza ingredients and incorporated them into this wonderful meatloaf. Serve it with a hearty red wine, and you'll feel as if you're dining in Rome!

SERVES 6 to 8

Sauce

1 10¾-ounce can tomato soup
¼ cup water

½ teaspoon dried oregano
1 small garlic clove, minced

Meatloaf

2 pounds ground beef
2 tablespoons chopped fresh
   parsley
1 large egg, lightly beaten

¼ cup chopped onion
1 teaspoon salt
½ teaspoon black pepper
1 cup cubed fresh bread*

Topping

2 slices mozzarella cheese

*If necessary, add more cubed bread a tablespoon at a time to make a firm loaf.

1. Preheat the oven to 350 degrees. Lightly oil a 10 × 13-inch baking dish.

2. In a small bowl, combine the soup, water, oregano, and garlic. Blend well.

3. In a large bowl, combine the meatloaf ingredients and add ¼ cup of the soup mixture. Mix well.

4. Form the mixture into a loaf and place in the prepared pan.

5. Bake for 1 hour and 15 minutes or until done.

6. Remove from the oven and drain the grease. Pour the rest of the soup mixture over the loaf.

7. Place slices of cheese on top. Bake until the cheese melts.

1991 FINALIST—THE GREAT AMERICAN MEATLOAF CONTEST, NORTHEAST REGIONAL COOKOFF

Spiced Lamb Loaf

ANNE FREDERICK
NEW HARTFORD, NEW YORK

"My favorite Greek restaurant in town features many lamb and eggplant dishes. My love of this combination inspired me to devise this meatloaf dish,"
—ANNE FREDERICK

SERVES 8

Meatloaf

3 tablespoons olive oil
1½ cups chopped eggplant
½ cup finely chopped onion
1 garlic clove, minced
2 teaspoons chili powder
¼ teaspoon ground cumin
¼ teaspoon ground coriander
1½ pounds ground lamb
1 cup chopped potato

⅓ cup seasoned bread crumbs*
2 tablespoons chopped green chilies
4 drops hot sauce
1 large egg, lightly beaten
⅓ cup chili sauce
¼ teaspoon salt
Cilantro leaves for garnish

*If necessary, add more bread crumbs a tablespoon at a time to make a firm loaf.

Cheese Sauce

2 tablespoons butter
3 tablespoons all-purpose flour
1 cup milk, at room
   temperature
2 tablespoons chili sauce
2 tablespoons chopped green
   chilies

2 tablespoons chopped
   scallions
2 drops hot sauce
3 ounces Monterey Jack
   cheese, cubed

1. Preheat the oven to 375 degrees. Lightly oil a 9 × 5 × 3-inch loaf pan.

2. In a large skillet, heat the olive oil over medium heat. Add the eggplant, onion, and garlic. Cook, stirring often, for 7 to 10 minutes, or until soft.

3. Stir in the chili powder, cumin, and coriander. Cook, stirring for 1 minute. Remove from the heat and cool slightly.

4. In a large bowl, mix the remaining meatloaf ingredients except the cilantro. Stir in the eggplant mixture.

5. Place the mixture in the prepared pan and bake for 45 minutes to 1 hour, or until done. Let the loaf sit for 10 minutes before slicing.

6. Meanwhile, in a saucepan, melt the butter over medium heat. Add the flour and stir for 30 seconds. Stir in the remaining ingredients except the cheese. Cook over medium to high heat for 3 to 4 minutes, stirring often. Add the cheese and cook until it melts.

7. Garnish the loaf with the cilantro leaves. Slice the meatloaf and serve with the cheese sauce.

Chapter 4

Meatloaf Roll-Ups

*M*eatloaf rolled up? Isn't that too much work? And is it technically still a meatloaf? If you're asking yourself these questions, read on.

There is a method to the madness. Fillings such as pesto, mushrooms, cheese, and spinach are better distributed throughout meatloaf by rolling it. Each slice then carries just the right amount of filling. From an aesthetic point of view, a colorful filling that spirals within each slice creates an attractive presentation. So you'll be comfortable serving it on your best platter and even slicing it at the table.

The roll-up method also works well in poultry loaf recipes. Try Pamela Seaman's prize-winning Chicken Cordon Bleu with Mushroom Sauce, which is featured in Chapter 7 (page 220) along with other great poultry roll-up recipes.

Now, back to the "Isn't it too much work?" Rolling up a meatloaf is as easy as rolling off a barrel . . . a very small barrel. We are the most un-jellyroll-like cooks around, and if we can do it, anyone can. Just follow these 53 steps (just kidding).

TIPS TO ROLL YOUR LOAF

After doing many meatloaf roll-ups, we came up with some techniques that may assist you. However, everyone has his or her own favorite method. At World Meatloaf Headquarters we roll meatloaves this way:

1. Lightly coat a large piece of aluminum foil with nonstick cooking spray or use vegetable oil. Place the lightly oiled piece of foil on a baking sheet.

2. Wet your hands, and place the meatloaf on the aluminum foil. Flatten the mixture and form into a rectangular shape. Depending on the size of the loaf, the actual dimensions of the rectangle will vary. Ideally, the mixture should be ½ inch thick when pressed out. This will allow enough mixture to surround your filling when you roll it up. (Tip: If you prefer not using your hands, either ask somebody else to do it or cover your hands with small plastic sandwich bags.)

3. Pour the filling mixture onto the middle of the loaf. Then spread the filling over the rectangle, leaving a 1½- to 2-inch border of uncovered meat. This will prevent the filling from spilling out the sides.

4. After the filling has been spread, place a piece of wax paper on top and refrigerate the unrolled meatloaf for 30 minutes. You will find it is much easier to roll when it is chilled.

5. Begin rolling the loaf from one of the short sides unless otherwise instructed in the recipe. Lift the foil as you roll the loaf.

6. When you have reached the end and you've formed the roll-up, wet your hands and crimp the ends of the loaf so the filling doesn't leak out. It's also a good idea to crimp the seam so the filling doesn't try to escape while cooking.

7. Place the loaf seam side down in a loaf pan. Use a pan that just fits the size of the loaf. This will keep the loaf from spreading out too much.

8. As we have suggested throughout the book, if you prefer the rolled loaf not to cook in its own fat you have two options: (a) use an aluminum foil pan and cut slits in the bottom, which will allow the grease from the loaf to drip through into another pan; (b) wrap the rolled loaf in aluminum foil. With a sharp knife, cut several slits in the bottom of the foil and place the wrapped loaf on a cooling rack. Place the cooling rack in another pan to catch the drippings.

Meatloaf Stuffed with Ham and Cheese

THOMAS E. MASSE
VERNON, CONNECTICUT

WMHQ Note: A well-seasoned beef roll-up with guts. Thomas used his mother's meatloaf recipe and embellished it with the ham and cheese.

SERVES 6

Meatloaf

1¼ pounds ground sirloin
1 large onion, finely chopped
1 teaspoon prepared mustard, preferably Dijon
1 10¾-ounce can tomato soup
2 tablespoons chopped fresh parsley
1 green bell pepper, finely chopped

2 large eggs, lightly beaten
1 cup plain bread crumbs*
⅛ teaspoon salt
⅛ teaspoon black pepper
1 garlic clove, minced
½ teaspoon dried oregano

Stuffing

6 thin slices boiled ham

1 cup shredded mozzarella cheese

*If necessary, add more bread crumbs a tablespoon at a time to make a firm loaf.

Topping

1 tablespoon all-purpose flour   3 slices mozzarella cheese

1. Preheat the oven to 400 degrees. Lightly oil a 9 × 5 × 3-inch loaf pan.

2. In a large bowl, combine the meatloaf ingredients. Lightly spray a large piece of aluminum foil. Place the meat mixture on the foil and form into a 12 × 8-inch rectangle. (See page 94 for roll-up instructions.)

3. Arrange the ham on top of the meat, leaving a small margin around the edges. Sprinkle shredded cheese on top of the ham slices.

4. Starting from the short end, carefully roll the meat mixture jelly-roll style. Seal the edges and ends.

5. Place the loaf seam side up in the prepared pan. Sprinkle the top of the meatloaf with the flour.

6. Bake 1 hour or until done. The center of the loaf will be pink because of the ham. Top the loaf with slices of the cheese, then return to the oven for 5 minutes or until the cheese melts. (Option: Broil the loaf to melt the cheese. Just watch it carefully!)

Uptown Beef Cake

———————•———————

Lorraine G. Carr
ROCHESTER, MASSACHUSETTS

WMHQ Note: This is a roll-up with a kick. The chili powder contrasts well with the topping. Like other Southwestern recipes, this blends the heat of the chili powder with the coolness of the sour cream. I don't mean to get mushy here, but it works.

Serves 6

Meatloaf

1½ pounds ground beef
¾ cup finely crushed Ritz
 crackers*
1 large egg, lightly beaten
1 tablespoon chili powder
1 tablespoon Worcestershire
 sauce

¼ cup canned chilies, drained
 and minced
6 ounces Monterey Jack
 cheese, shredded
½ cup chopped onion

Sauce

1½ cups sour cream or yogurt

1 teaspoon prepared
 horseradish or to taste

*If necessary, add more cracker crumbs a tablespoon at a time to make a firm loaf.

Topping and Garnish

3 tablespoons butter
4 cherry tomatoes

2 cups fresh white bread
    crumbs
¼ cup grated Romano cheese

1. Preheat the oven to 350 degrees. Lightly oil a 9 × 12 × 2-inch baking pan.

2. In a large bowl, combine the beef, crackers, egg, chili powder, Worcestershire sauce, and minced chilies.

3. Wet your hands and flatten the meat mixture into a 10 × 12-inch rectangle on a piece of wax paper. (See page 94 for roll-up instructions.)

4. Sprinkle the cheese and onion on top of the meat mixture, leaving a 1-inch margin on all sides. Roll up the loaf jellyroll fashion. Press the ends together and seal. Place the loaf seam side down in the prepared pan.

5. Cook for 1 hour. Drain the fat and return the loaf to the oven for 10 minutes, or until done.

6. In a small bowl, combine the sour cream or yogurt and horseradish. Set aside.

7. In a large skillet, melt the butter. Briefly cook the whole cherry tomatoes until glazed. Remove the tomatoes from the skillet, reserving the remaining butter.

8. In the same skillet, heat the bread crumbs and cheese until golden brown (add more butter if needed).

9. Place the rolled loaf on a serving platter. Coat with the sour cream sauce and sprinkle with toasted bread crumbs. Garnish with the glazed cherry tomatoes.

Stuffed Meatloaf Lithuanian Style

BARBARA A. REICHERT

FAIRFIELD, CONNECTICUT

WMHQ Note: The flavorful stuffing in Barbara's recipe made this loaf a favorite at World Meatloaf Headquarters. We've made it again, even after the judging was over.

SERVES 6 to 8

Meatloaf

1 pound lean ground beef
½ pound ground turkey
½ pound ground veal or pork
1 large egg white
½ cup fresh Italian or French
    bread crumbs*
¼ cup wheat germ
¼ cup oat bran

2 tablespoons grated Parmesan
    cheese
⅛ teaspoon salt
½ cup evaporated skim milk
1 small onion, finely chopped
1 tablespoon minced garlic, or
    ¼ teaspoon garlic powder
⅛ teaspoon black pepper

Stuffing

40 low-salt saltine crackers,
    coarsely crushed
1 large egg, lightly beaten
¼ teaspoon poultry seasoning
    or Bell's Stuffing herbs

⅔ cup low-salt canned chicken
    broth

*If necessary, add more bread crumbs a tablespoon at a time to make a firm loaf.

1. Preheat the oven to 350 degrees. Lightly coat a 9 × 5 × 3-inch loaf pan with nonstick spray.

2. In a large bowl, combine the meatloaf ingredients. Mix thoroughly and set aside in the refrigerator for 30 minutes, giving the flavors time to blend.

3. In another bowl, combine the stuffing ingredients and set aside.

4. Place the meatloaf mixture on a large piece of wax paper. Flatten the meatloaf mixture into a large rectangle.

5. Spread the stuffing mixture on top of the meat, leaving a 2-inch border. Starting with the short side of the rectangle, roll up like a jelly roll. Seal the sides and edges well. (See page 94 for roll-up instructions.)

6. Place the rolled loaf seam side down in the prepared pan.

7. Bake the meatloaf for 1 hour. Drain off any excess fat from the pan and return to the oven for 15 minutes or until done. Let the loaf sit for 10 minutes before slicing.

A Baby Swiss Meatloaf

———————————— • ————————————

DOROTHY BEYER

ST. PETERSBURG BEACH, FLORIDA

WMHQ Note: This recipe has a great blend of flavors. One of the interesting features is the Baby Swiss cheese. You can tell it's baby cheese because it has little, tiny holes, not the mature holes of its parent. A little more than you wanted to know, wasn't it?

SERVES 6 to 8

Sauce

¼ cup diced Ro-Tel Tomato &
  Green Chilies*
¼ cup ketchup
1 teaspoon dry mustard

¾ tablespoon light brown
  sugar, packed
¼ teaspoon grated nutmeg

Filling

4 cups shredded zucchini
  (spinach may be
  substituted)
4 garlic cloves, finely diced
3 tablespoons vegetable oil
½ teaspoon garlic salt

¼ cup grated Parmesan cheese
1 cup shredded Baby Swiss
  cheese
½ cup Italian-flavored bread
  crumbs†

*If you can't find this, use canned tomatoes and canned green chilies. Dice them and combine.
†If necessary, add more bread crumbs a tablespoon at a time to make a firm loaf.

Meatloaf

1 pound ground beef
½ pound ground pork
½ pound ground veal
½ cup grated onion
1 teaspoon dried thyme
¼ teaspoon onion powder
1 cup diced Ro-Tel Tomato &
   Green Chilies*

¼ teaspoon black pepper
⅛ teaspoon dried hot red
   pepper flakes (optional)
¼ cup sliced green olives
   stuffed with pimientos

Topping

4 to 6 strips bacon, uncooked

1. Preheat the oven to 350 degrees. Lightly spray a cooling rack with nonstick cooking spray. Place the rack in a roasting pan.

2. In a small bowl, mix the sauce ingredients and put aside.

3. In a medium skillet, cook the zucchini and 1 diced garlic clove in the oil, stirring constantly and draining if necessary.

4. To the skillet add ¼ teaspoon garlic salt, Parmesan cheese, Baby Swiss cheese, and bread crumbs. Mix well and set aside to cool.

5. In another bowl, combine the ground meats with the grated onion and the rest of the garlic. Add the rest of the spices, the diced tomatoes and green chilies, and the pepper flakes. Mix well.

6. On a large piece of wax paper, form the meat mixture into a 10- to 12-inch square. (See page 94 for roll-up instructions.)

7. Spread the cooled zucchini mixture on top of the meat, leaving a 1-inch border around the edges.

(*continued*)

---

*If you can't find this, use canned tomatoes and canned green chilies. Dice them and combine.

8. Spread the sliced olives over the zucchini. Roll the mixture jelly-roll fashion and seal the seams. Place the loaf seam side down on the cooling rack.

9. Lay the bacon strips over the top, tucking the edges under.

10. Spread the sauce over the top. Bake for 1 to 1½ hours, or until done.

A Bachelor's "Better Than Steak" Meatloaf

—————————•—————————

Jean McCormick
SHOAL CREEK, ALABAMA

WMHQ Note: This meatloaf was inspired by Jean's son Greg. The use of sourdough French bread as a binder gave it a chewy consistency. For those of you who aren't big blue cheese fans, give this loaf a chance. To serve, cut the other half of the sourdough loaf into slices and spread butter on each piece. Sprinkle garlic powder on top of each slice and broil until brown.

SERVES 8 to 10

Meat Mixture

1 small white onion, minced
2 garlic cloves, minced
6 to 8 fresh basil leaves,
  minced
2 large eggs, lightly beaten
⅛ teaspoon salt
⅛ teaspoon black pepper

8 to 10 drops Worcestershire
  sauce
2½ pounds ground beef
1¼ pounds ground veal
¾ pound ground mild pork
  sausage

Filling

½ small loaf sourdough
  French bread
½ cup half-and-half

1 cup crumbled blue cheese
3 tablespoons minced fresh
  parsley

1. Preheat the oven to 375 degrees. Lightly oil a cookie sheet with sides.

2. In a large bowl, combine the onion, garlic, basil, eggs, salt, pepper, and Worcestershire sauce. Add the meats to the mixture and blend well.

3. On a piece of plastic wrap, form the meat mixture into a 13-inch rectangle ½ inch thick. (See page 94 for roll-up instructions.)

4. Soak the bread in the half-and-half. Squeeze out very well. Spread the bread over the meat layer.

5. Spread the blue cheese over the bread layer.

6. Sprinkle the parsley over the cheese.

7. Roll up the meat mixture jellyroll fashion and remove the plastic wrap. Seal both ends. Place the meatloaf on the prepared cookie sheet.

8. Bake for 1 hour or until done. Let the loaf sit for 10 minutes before serving.

1991 Second Place—The Great American Meatloaf Contest, Northeast Regional Cookoff

Rolled Meatloaf with Mushroom–Goat Cheese Stuffing

Turi Hoffman

COS COB, CONNECTICUT

WMHQ Note: Turi's recipe is terrific. When I was asked to be on ''Live with Regis and Kathie Lee,'' I made this recipe the day before the appearance in the studio's kitchen. After the segment, I brought all of the 1991 winning recipes I had prepared back to the green room (which also doubles as the office for the backstage crew), and this loaf was devoured in about 2 minutes.

Serves 6

Stuffing

2 tablespoons butter
1 tablespoon olive oil
2 large garlic cloves, finely
  chopped
2 shallots, finely chopped
1 teaspoon fresh thyme, or ½
  teaspoon dried

1 pound fresh mushrooms,
  stems removed, halved, and
  sliced
1 tablespoon chopped fresh
  sage, or 1 teaspoon dried
½ teaspoon salt
½ teaspoon black pepper

Meat Mixture

1 pound ground beef
1 pound ground veal
2 large eggs, lightly beaten
½ cup plain bread crumbs*
½ cup grated Pecorino
   Romano cheese

¼ cup ketchup
1 tablespoon Dijon mustard
½ cup chopped fresh parsley
⅛ teaspoon hot sauce
1 teaspoon salt
½ teaspoon black pepper

Filling

3½ ounces goat cheese, at
   room temperature

1. Preheat the oven to 350 degrees. Lightly oil a 9 × 5 × 3-inch loaf pan.

2. In a large skillet, heat 1 tablespoon butter and the olive oil over moderately low heat. Add the garlic, shallots, and thyme, stirring once or twice, about 2 minutes. Increase the heat to moderately high and stir in the mushrooms. Cover and cook until the mushrooms soften, stirring once, about 4 minutes. Remove the cover and add the sage, salt, pepper, and the remaining 1 tablespoon butter. Cook, stirring until lightly browned, about 3 to 4 minutes. Set aside.

3. In a large bowl, combine the beef and veal. Stir in the eggs, bread crumbs, grated cheese, ketchup, mustard, parsley, hot sauce, salt, and pepper. Mix well.

4. Spread the meat mixture onto a sheet of wax paper to approximately 8 × 16 inches, so when rolled it will fit into the loaf pan. Spread the goat cheese over the meat mixture, and spread the mushroom stuffing evenly over the goat cheese. Carefully lift the

(*continued*)

---

*If necessary, add more bread crumbs a tablespoon at a time to make a firm loaf.

wax paper from the shorter side, and using it as a guide, roll up the meat like a jellyroll, pressing gently and peeling the paper off as you roll. (See page 94 for roll-up instructions.) Place the rolled meatloaf into the prepared loaf pan with the seam of the meatloaf on the bottom.

5. Bake the meatloaf for 1 hour and 15 minutes or until done. Let the loaf stand, covered lightly, for 15 minutes before slicing and serving.

Tante Cha's Magnifique Meatloaf

CHA GRENN

LAS VEGAS, NEVADA

WMHQ Note: This loaf blends the popular North African ingredient couscous with an array of exotic flavors. The sauce features molasses, which is always a lot of fun to work with. But be careful pouring the molasses because, like honey, if it slides down the side of the jar, you might spend the rest of the day trying to get it off everything it touches—like your counter, your guests, or your hair.

SERVES 8

Couscous

¼ cup water
⅛ teaspoon salt

½ tablespoon butter
¼ cup instant couscous

Filling

2 tablespoons butter
1 tablespoon olive oil
⅓ cup chopped shallots
½ pound fresh mushrooms,
   washed, dried, and sliced

¼ teaspoon salt
½ teaspoon black pepper
⅓ cup chopped black olives
½ cup shredded Swiss cheese
¼ cup chopped fresh parsley

Meatloaf

1 pound lean ground sirloin
½ pound ground pork
1 strip bacon, cooked until
   well done and crumbled
2 tablespoons Worcestershire
   sauce
⅓ cup low-fat milk

⅓ cup Marsala wine
2 large eggs, beaten well
⅛ teaspoon garlic powder
⅛ teaspoon mace
1 teaspoon onion powder
½ teaspoon salt
⅛ teaspoon dried savory

Sauce

½ cup ketchup
2 tablespoons molasses
1 teaspoon Dijon mustard
1 teaspoon garlic wine
   vinegar*

¼ teaspoon ground allspice
⅓ cup slivered almonds

1. Preheat the oven to 350 degrees. Lightly oil a 9 × 5 × 3-inch loaf pan.

2. In a small saucepan, bring the water, salt, and butter to a boil. Stir in the couscous.† Cover and remove from the heat and let stand for 5 minutes. Fluff with a fork before combining with the loaf mixture.

(continued)

---

*If you don't have garlic wine vinegar, combine ⅛ teaspoon garlic powder in ½ cup white or red wine vinegar and mix thoroughly. Use 1 teaspoon in the recipe and you can use the rest on a tossed salad and serve it with the meatloaf.

†If necessary, add more cooked couscous a tablespoon at a time to make a firm loaf.

3. In a medium skillet over high heat, combine the butter and oil. When hot, add the shallots and mushrooms. Sauté for 4 minutes.

4. Add the salt, pepper, and black olives. Sauté for another minute. As soon as the mushrooms have browned lightly, remove from the heat and place in a bowl to cool. Stir the Swiss cheese and parsley into the shallot-mushroom mixture.

5. Using an electric mixer, combine the couscous with the meats. Add all remaining ingredients and mix well.

6. Measure out a piece of plastic wrap approximately 12 × 16 inches. Spread the meatloaf mixture on it, forming a rectangle. Spread the filling on top of the meat mixture and roll jellyroll style. Seal the edges. Place in the prepared pan with the seam on the bottom. (See page 94 for roll-up instructions.)

7. In a medium bowl, mix the ketchup, molasses, mustard, vinegar, allspice, and almonds. Spoon the sauce on the meatloaf to cover. Place the loaf pan on a cookie sheet with sides.

8. Bake for 1 hour and 15 minutes or until done. Let the loaf sit for 10 minutes before slicing.

Meatloaf Sempre Buono

◆

Marilyn T. Sandonato

NORTH SCITUATE, MASSACHUSETTS

WMHQ Note: This is a delicious loaf accompanied by a homemade Italian tomato sauce. You might want to double the recipe for the sauce and serve leftover meatloaf with pasta at another time. However, if the bowling team is on its way over for dinner in an hour, you can substitute your favorite brand of commercial spaghetti sauce.

Serves 8

Tomato Sauce

¼ cup olive oil
2 tablespoons finely minced onion
2 tablespoons finely minced fresh parsley
2 garlic cloves, finely minced
1 35-ounce can Italian plum tomatoes

1 8-ounce can tomato sauce
4 fresh basil leaves, chopped, or 1 teaspoon dried
⅛ teaspoon dried oregano
⅛ teaspoon salt
⅛ teaspoon black pepper

Meatloaf

½ pound sweet Italian sausage, casing removed
2 pounds ground sirloin
2 tablespoons finely minced onion
2 tablespoons finely minced fresh parsley

1 garlic clove, finely minced
¼ cup grated Romano cheese
⅛ teaspoon salt
⅛ teaspoon black pepper
2 large eggs, lightly beaten
1 cup Italian-flavored bread crumbs*

(continued)

*If necessary, add more bread crumbs a tablespoon at a time to make a firm loaf.

Filling

1 10-ounce package frozen
  spinach, thawed and
  drained
½ cup grated Provolone cheese

½ cup thinly sliced fresh
  mushrooms

Topping

½ cup grated Provolone cheese

1. Preheat the oven to 350 degrees. Lightly oil an 8 × 15 × 3-inch roasting pan.

2. In a medium saucepan, heat the olive oil. Add the onion, parsley, and garlic and cook over medium heat until the mixture is soft but not brown, about 3 to 4 minutes.

3. Remove the pan from the heat. Place a food mill over the pan and empty the tomatoes into it. Process the tomatoes through the food mill to remove any skin and seeds.

4. Add the tomato sauce, basil, oregano, salt, and pepper. Simmer for 25 minutes over medium-low heat.

5. Measure ½ cup of the sauce for the meatloaf mixture and reserve the remaining sauce.

6. Place the sausage in a food processor and process with the steel blade for 30 seconds.

7. In a large bowl, combine the sausage, sirloin, onion, parsley, garlic, cheese, salt, pepper, eggs, ½ cup tomato sauce, and bread crumbs. Mix well.

8. Place the meat mixture on a large piece of wax paper. Shape the mixture into a rectangle approximately 10 × 16 inches.

9. Squeeze the drained spinach between paper towels to remove excess moisture. With a sharp knife, chop the spinach. Spread the spinach over the rectangle, leaving a 1-inch border all around. Sprinkle the Provolone cheese and mushrooms over the spinach.

10. Roll the meat mixture by lifting the wax paper from the shorter side and peeling the paper off as you roll the loaf. (See page 94 for roll-up instructions.)

11. Place the mixture seam side down in the prepared roasting pan. Seal the ends of the loaf. Bake for 1 hour.

12. Remove the pan from the oven and pour the remaining tomato sauce over the loaf. Return to the oven for 20 minutes, basting twice with the tomato sauce.

13. Sprinkle the topping cheese on top of the loaf and return to the oven to melt the cheese.

14. Let the loaf sit for 10 minutes before serving. Place slices of the meatloaf in the center of the plates and spoon the tomato sauce around the edges of the slices.

Chapter 5

Meatloaves with a Kick

T hese recipes are proof positive that Southwestern cooking is big. Really big. As a matter of fact, salsa outsells ketchup in the United States. The recipes in this chapter are excellent examples of incorporating Southwestern flair in basic meatloaf recipes.

Want a great recipe for salsa? See page 125 for Mickey Strang's Spicy Meatloaf with Homemade Salsa. You'll find some of these meatloaf recipes may have more kick than you'd like. Reduce the number of chilies or peppers and/or use mild salsa to cut the heat. On the other hand, if you want your loaf hotter, add more chilies or chili powder.

Several recipes use canned chilies. You'll find others call for fresh chilies. Fresh chilies are usually available in the produce section of your supermarket. If you can't find any, feel free to use canned.

To prepare fresh chilies for a recipe, use a sharp paring knife to remove the seeds and the core. Make sure all the seeds are removed—that's where the heat is concentrated. Then slice or mince the pepper according to the recipe directions. You may want to wear gloves when handling hot peppers!

L. M. Lacey's New Mexico Green Chili Meatloaf (page 127) uses roasted chili peppers. It is very simple to roast your own peppers: Use the following method for roasting fresh chili peppers or bell peppers.

1. Using a long-handled fork or skewer, place the peppers directly over a gas flame. Or place the peppers on a rack under the broiler. If you use the broiler, get the peppers as close to the flame as possible.

2. Turn the peppers until they are charred on all sides.

3. Place the charred peppers in a paper bag and close tightly. Let them sit for 10 minutes.

4. After 10 minutes, shake the bag. The charred skin should fall off easily. Wearing rubber gloves, remove the peppers from the bag and use a sharp knife to remove any skin still on the peppers. You can also rinse them under cold water, then use a knife to remove the stem and seeds.

You can place roasted peppers in foil and freeze them for future use. Or, wrap them and refrigerate to use within a few days.

On the Side

I'll never forget the first time I tried a Southwestern meatloaf. It seems like only yesterday.

In 1983, my friend Dan and I took a trip cross-country by train, eventually ending up on a six-day rafting trip on the Colorado River through the Grand Canyon. After sitting straight up, staring out the window for three days and two nights (because Dan forgot to book a sleeper), the last thing I was ready for was the rigors of a rafting trip.

The thrill of munching on trail mix and sleeping under the stars lasted one night, but I had five more to go. I asked Dan about the rest of the trip. "It's all taken care of," he assured me. "When we climb out of here, we'll be staying at a hotel at the top of the Canyon."

At 9 A.M. it was already 122 degrees. A soft bed, a hot shower, and a cold meatloaf sandwich with a frosty mug of beer were the thoughts that kept me putting one foot in front of the other up that long trail. Eleven hours and 23 pints of water later, we emerged at the top. Never had a hotel looked so good. Too bad Dan hadn't guaranteed the hotel reservation.

The next day we made our way to Kingman, Arizona, to take a bus back to Flagstaff. The bus station in Kingman is small, and we knew that our chances of messing up this part of the trip were slim. But not slim enough. There was one more bus going to Flagstaff, and the woman behind the counter assured us that we couldn't miss it. We had forty-five minutes to kill, so I spent the time telling Dan how much I appreciated the skill in which he had managed the trip so far. I even suggested that he look into a career in the travel business.

A while later the woman behind the counter looked at us and said, "You boys still here? I thought you wanted to be on the bus to Flagstaff? It left 10 minutes ago."

Hitchhiking was the last chance we had to get to Flagstaff to catch the train back home. We were unshaven, sunburned, tired, and aggravated. After three hours of walking backwards, our thumbs pointing toward Flagstaff, a red pickup truck pulled over. "I only have room for one of you up front, so one of you will have to ride in the back," the driver said.

There I was sitting with twelve of the biggest, smelliest sheep I had ever had the pleasure to know. Wedged in among thousands of pounds of future sweaters (and lamb chops), I started to rethink this whole adventure idea.

"Well," Dan yelled over the bleating. "At least we'll have a story to tell everyone when we get back home." He was still laughing at the thought of my getting out of the pickup truck covered with sheep droppings. "Let's clean up and get some dinner. It's on me," he offered magnanimously.

We walked across the street to a diner. "This looks like a good place. What could go wrong?" he asked innocently. I had my long awaited Southwestern meatloaf sandwich and a frosty mug of beer. Dan had the "trucker's mixed grill." To this day, he's still trying to figure out what it was mixed with. As we walked toward a convenience store after dinner, a strange look came over Dan's face. "Are you OK?" I asked him. "I think I ate something bad. Real bad," he told me. Dan ran (or waddled) the remaining quarter-mile to the convenience store. I entered the store a few minutes later and asked the man behind the counter if a pale, sweating lawyer had just waddled in. "Oh sure, he's in the back getting sick." Sure enough, Dan had learned something: When you're on the road in a strange town, in a strange restaurant, always order the meatloaf!

Tex-Mex Chili Meatloaf

•

Pat Sprankle

NASHUA, NEW HAMPSHIRE

WMHQ Note: This is a loaf with a lot of good stuff in it: corn, pinto beans, jalapeños, and tomatoes. If you're really feeling creative, you can arrange the corn to spell out your dinner companion's name when you slice the loaf. (Only recommended when you have NOTHING else to do.)

Meatloaf

1 tablespoon olive oil
1 medium onion, coarsely
  chopped
1 red bell pepper, coarsely
  chopped
2 garlic cloves, minced
1 fresh jalapeño pepper, cored,
  seeded, and minced
1 teaspoon salt
2 tablespoons chili powder
2 teaspoons ground cumin

2 teaspoons dried basil
1 28-ounce can whole
  tomatoes, drained and cut
  into chunks
1 8-ounce can tomato sauce
2 pounds lean ground beef
2 large eggs, lightly beaten
1 cup plain bread crumbs*
1 cup canned pinto beans,
  rinsed and drained
¾ cup canned corn, drained

Sauce

1 16-ounce jar thick and
  chunky salsa

Garnish

Fresh cilantro   Bottled hot red peppers

1. Preheat the oven to 350 degrees. Lightly oil a 3-quart baking dish.

2. Heat the oil in a 10-inch frying pan and sauté the onion and red bell pepper until soft, about 4 to 6 minutes. Add the garlic and jalapeño and sauté 1 minute more. Remove from the heat.

3. Add the salt, chili powder, cumin, and basil, mixing well. Stir in the tomatoes and tomato sauce, and mix again; set aside.

(*continued*)

*If necessary, add more bread crumbs a tablespoon at a time to make a firm loaf.

4. In a large bowl, combine the ground beef, eggs, and bread crumbs; add the tomato mixture and mix well.

5. Mix in the beans and corn.

6. Transfer the meat mixture to the prepared baking dish and form into a flat loaf.

7. Bake the meatloaf for 1 hour or until the thermometer inserted in the center of the loaf registers 160 degrees.

8. Heat the salsa in a small saucepan and keep warm.

9. Pour off the drippings and let the meatloaf sit for 10 minutes. Transfer the meatloaf to a serving platter. Garnish with the cilantro and hot peppers.

10. Cut the meatloaf into slices. Spoon some of the salsa onto serving plates and place meatloaf slices on top. Serve immediately.

Mexicana Fire Loaf

ANNE P. SMITH
CRANSTON, RHODE ISLAND

"This recipe came about after a gathering in my home which left me with an abundance of salsa and cheese. My husband just loves meatloaf, so I decided to experiment with my leftovers. After refiguring my measurements, he found this recipe much to his liking. He does suggest that ice water be kept handy to cool down the fire."   —ANNE SMITH

SERVES 6

Meatloaf

1½ pounds lean ground beef
¾ cup seasoned bread crumbs*
¼ cup finely chopped fresh
  jalapeño pepper†
⅓ cup finely chopped celery
⅓ cup finely chopped onion

⅓ cup medium-hot chunky
  salsa†
1 large egg, lightly beaten
¼ teaspoon ground cumin
¼ teaspoon garlic powder

Sauce

1 cup medium-hot salsa,†
  warmed

½ cup shredded Monterey
  Jack cheese or Monterey
  Jack with jalapeño

1. Preheat the oven to 350 degrees. Lightly oil a 9 × 5 × 3-inch loaf pan.

2. In a large bowl, combine the ground beef, bread crumbs, jalapeño pepper, celery, and onion. Mix well.

3. In a small bowl, mix the salsa, egg, cumin, and garlic. Add to the meat mixture. Blend thoroughly.

4. Press the meatloaf mixture into the prepared loaf pan.

5. Bake for 1 hour or until done. Drain off any grease and let the meatloaf sit for 10 minutes. Turn out the loaf onto a warm platter.

6. Spread the warm salsa over the loaf before serving and sprinkle with the shredded cheese.

---

*If necessary, add more bread crumbs a tablespoon at a time to make a firm loaf.
†You may turn the fire up or cool down the recipe by using either mild or hot salsa and another type of chili pepper.

Meatloaf Olé

•

Edward R. Felesky
LAS VEGAS, NEVADA

WMHQ Note: This meatloaf will start your engines. The corn chips or tortilla chips are terrific binders.

Serves 8

Topping

1½ cups tomato paste
⅛ cup sugar
½ teaspoon cayenne pepper

½ teaspoon salt
½ teaspoon black pepper

Meatloaf

2½ pounds ground beef
2 cups tomatoes, chopped, or 1
   1 14½-ounce can chopped
   tomatoes
½ green bell pepper, seeded
   and finely chopped
1 medium onion, finely
   chopped
½ cup very finely crushed
   tortilla or corn chips*

1 tablespoon fresh jalapeño
   pepper, seeded and finely
   chopped
2 garlic cloves, minced
½ teaspoon ground cumin
1½ teaspoons salt
½ teaspoon dried oregano
1 teaspoon black pepper
¼ cup chopped fresh cilantro
2 large eggs, lightly beaten

*If necessary, add more chip crumbs a tablespoon at a time to make a firm loaf.

1. Preheat the oven to 350 degrees. Lightly oil a 9 × 13-inch baking pan.

2. In a small bowl, mix the topping ingredients and set aside.

3. In a separate bowl, combine the meat, tomatoes, bell pepper, onion, chips, jalapeño, garlic, seasonings, and 3 tablespoons of the topping.

4. Add eggs, mix well, and shape into a loaf.

5. Place the meatloaf in the prepared baking pan. Bake 50 minutes.

6. Spread on the remaining topping and bake 10 minutes more, or until a meat thermometer reaches 150 to 160 degrees. Let the loaf sit for 10 minutes before slicing.

Southwestern Meatloaf

●

MARY L. MILLER

SAN GABRIEL, CALIFORNIA

WMHQ Note: If you want a quick, spicy meatloaf, here it is. The Mexicorn has a lot of flavor and the chili powder gives it a kick. Never rub your eyes after handling chilies or chili powder. It tends to sting.

SERVES 6

1½ pounds lean ground beef
½ cup Italian-flavored bread
  crumbs*
1 large egg, lightly beaten
½ cup ketchup

1 envelope (0.9 ounce) onion
  soup mix
1 6-ounce can Mexicorn
  drained†
1 tablespoon chili powder

1. Preheat the oven to 350 degrees. Lightly oil a 9 × 5 × 3-inch loaf pan.

2. In a large bowl, combine all the ingredients and mix well. Place the meatloaf mixture in the prepared loaf pan.

3. Bake uncovered for 45 minutes to 1 hour, or until done. Let the meatloaf sit for 15 minutes before slicing. If desired, before serving, add salsa on top for a zestier taste.

---

*If necessary, add more bread a few pieces at a time to make a firm loaf.
†If you can't find Mexicorn, combine 1 tablespoon of diced red bell pepper with a small can of corn. To make it with a kick, add a few drops of hot sauce to taste, or leave as is for a milder flavor.

Spicy Meatloaf with Homemade Salsa

MICKEY STRANG
McKINLEYVILLE, CALIFORNIA

WMHQ Note: This is a dynamite salsa! Make extra and keep it around to serve with chips, or top meatloaf sandwiches or hamburgers with it. When you put the extra salsa in the refrigerator, label it ''hot'' unless you want Aunt Gertie clutching her throat and trying to scream ''Water!'' at 2 o'clock in the morning.

SERVES 6

Meatloaf

1½ pounds lean ground beef
1 cup fresh, soft bread crumbs*
½ cup tomato juice
1 fresh jalapeño pepper, finely minced (about 1 tablespoon)

2 tablespoons minced onion
1 teaspoon dried oregano

Homemade Salsa

1½ cups peeled, seeded, and finely chopped ripe tomatoes
1 fresh jalapeño pepper, minced (about 1 tablespoon)

6 scallions (including the green part), finely chopped
1 tablespoon lime juice

(*continued*)

*If necessary, add more bread crumbs a tablespoon at a time to make a firm loaf.

Topping

½ cup sour cream   ¼ teaspoon dried hot red
                                      pepper flakes

Optional Garnish

Cilantro sprigs   Sliced black olives

1. Preheat the oven to 350 degrees. Lightly oil a 9-inch round casserole dish.

2. In a large bowl, combine the meat, bread crumbs, and tomato juice. Add the jalapeño, onion, and oregano.

3. Form into a loaf and place in the prepared casserole, allowing a 1-inch space all the way around. If you use the olive garnish, press them around the rim of the meatloaf to make a decorative pattern.

4. Bake for about 45 minutes to 1 hour, or until done.

5. While the meatloaf is baking, combine the salsa ingredients in a glass or ceramic bowl and leave at room temperature so the flavors can blend.

6. In a small bowl, mix the sour cream and crushed red pepper. Cover and refrigerate until ready to serve.

7. When the meatloaf is done, let it sit for 10 minutes and then remove it to a warm platter. Pour the salsa around the meatloaf.

8. Top the meatloaf with the sour cream–red pepper mix. Garnish with cilantro sprigs if you wish. Serve at once.

New Mexico Green Chili Meatloaf

●─────────

L. M. LACEY

AZTEC, NEW MEXICO

WMHQ Note: This recipe calls for roasted peppers; see page 116. This is a hot loaf, so if you want to tone down the heat, use fewer chili peppers.

S E R V E S 4

12 saltine crackers, crumbled*
½ cup milk
1 pound lean ground beef
½ cup diced onion
3 roasted green chili peppers,
    peeled and chopped
1 teaspoon salt

2 garlic cloves, chopped
1 cup grated cheese (Monterey
    Jack or sharp cheddar)
2 large eggs, lightly beaten
Parsley or watercress sprigs for
    garnish (optional)

1. Preheat the oven to 350 degrees. Lightly oil a 9 × 5 × 3-inch loaf pan.

2. In a small bowl, soak the crackers in milk.

3. In a large bowl, combine the remaining ingredients and add the cracker and milk mixture. Mix well. Press the meatloaf mixture into the prepared pan.

4. Bake for 1 to 1½ hours, or until done.

5. Let the loaf cool for 10 minutes before slicing.

6. Remove the loaf to a serving platter and garnish with parsley or watercress sprigs.

*If necessary, add more cracker crumbs a tablespoon at a time to make a firm loaf.

South of the Border Meatloaf

—————•—————

Jane Wyche
TAMPA, FLORIDA

WMHQ Note: This loaf tastes like nachos without the chips. Guys love nacho chips. Couches do also. You can't watch a ball game and eat a bag of chips without half the bag ending up between the cushions of the couch. You and your couch will appreciate this loaf.

Serves 6

Meatloaf

1½ pounds ground sirloin
½ cup chopped onion
⅔ cup rolled oats*
1 large egg, lightly beaten
1 tablespoon chili powder
½ teaspoon ground cumin

½ teaspoon black pepper
1 teaspoon salt
¼ teaspoon garlic powder
½ cup salsa, canned or
    homemade (page 125)

Filling

½ cup shredded cheddar
  cheese

*If necessary, add more oats a tablespoon at a time to make a firm loaf.

Topping

½ cup salsa   ½ cup shredded cheddar
cheese

1. Preheat the oven to 350 degrees. Lightly oil a 9 × 5 × 3-inch loaf pan.

2. In a large bowl, combine all the meatloaf ingredients. Mix well.

3. Pack half the meat mixture into the prepared pan. Sprinkle the shredded cheese over the meat.

4. Cover with the remaining meat mixture. Pour topping salsa over the top.

5. Cook for 50 minutes. Then sprinkle the topping cheese over the meatloaf and cook for 10 minutes. Let the loaf sit for 10 minutes before slicing.

Bloody Mary Meatloaf

———•———

FRED RAU

BURLINGTON, CONNECTICUT

"We're a big meatloaf family. . . . This meatloaf was the creation of four friends who like to get silly and eat meatloaf together." —FRED RAU

WMHQ Note: This really does taste like a Bloody Mary! When we made the loaf a second time, we increased the amount of horseradish, hot sauce, and celery salt. It really packed a wallop.

SERVES 6

2 pounds ground beef
1 large egg, lightly beaten
2 slices bread, processed into crumbs in a food processor or blender*
¼ cup finely chopped celery
½ cup tomato puree
2 tablespoons vodka
1 tablespoon fresh lime juice

1 teaspoon celery salt
1½ tablespoons prepared horseradish
3 drops hot sauce
2 teaspoons Worcestershire sauce
Celery tops with leaves for garnish

1. Preheat the oven to 350 degrees. Lightly oil a 9 × 5 × 3-inch loaf pan.

2. In a large bowl, combine all the ingredients. Mix well.

*If necessary, add more bread crumbs a tablespoon at a time to make a firm loaf.

3. Place the meat mixture into the prepared pan.

4. Bake for 1¼ hours or until done.

5. Let the loaf sit for 10 minutes. Then remove it a serving platter and garnish with celery leaves.

Mexican Bull Ring

Barbara Nowakowski

NORTH TONAWANDA, NEW YORK

WMHQ Note: Muy bueno. *The Colby cheese and the crushed nacho chips worked well together. We used medium-hot salsa, but adjust the heat to your taste.*

Serves 6

Meatloaf

2 cups crushed tortilla chips*
2½ pounds ground beef
1 12-ounce jar picante sauce,
   mild, medium, or hot

¼ teaspoon garlic powder
1¼ cups cubed Colby cheese
⅛ teaspoon salt
⅛ teaspoon black pepper

(*continued*)

*If necessary, add more chip crumbs a tablespoon at a time to make a firm loaf.

Topping

1 12-ounce jar picante sauce,
   mild, medium, or hot

1. Preheat the oven to 325 degrees. Lightly coat a 9-cup Bundt pan with nonstick cooking spray.

2. In a large bowl, combine the crushed chips, ground beef, ½ jar of picante sauce, garlic powder, cheese, salt, and pepper. Mix until well blended.

3. Place the meatloaf mixture into the prepared pan.

4. Bake for 1 hour. Drain the grease from the pan; top with the remaining picante sauce. Bake for another 30 minutes. Let the loaf sit for 10 minutes before slicing.

5. Right before the loaf is done baking, empty the jar of picante sauce into a small saucepan and heat. Top individual slices of meatloaf with the sauce.

Hot and Sassy Meatloaf

•

RONALD J. BLANK
NORTHAMPTON, MASSACHUSETTS

WMHQ Note: When I first saw the word sassy, *I said to myself, "What could possibly make a meatloaf sassy? Does it talk back? Is this meatloaf a teenager with a phone growing out of its ear? Am I thinking too much about this?" After tasting the loaf, I figured out that the mixture of peperoncino and hoisin sauce make the loaf hot and sassy (a word I've never used before). It's a terrific loaf.*

SERVES 6

Meatloaf

1 pound ground beef
¼ pound ground veal or pork
½ teaspoon salt
½ teaspoon black pepper
1 tablespoon chopped onion
1 large egg, lightly beaten
2 tablespoons chopped red or
    green bell pepper
¼ cup chopped black olives

2 medium peperoncino,*
    chopped
¼ cup diced water chestnuts
¾ cup crushed cornflakes†
¾ teaspoon chili powder
2 teaspoons hoisin sauce
¼ cup grated cheddar cheese
½ teaspoon minced garlic

Topping

2 tablespoons hoisin sauce

¼ cup crushed corn chips

(*continued*)

---

*Peperoncino is a hot red chili pepper available either fresh or dried. If you can't find this chili, substitute a jalapeño or other chili pepper.
†If necessary, add more cereal crumbs a tablespoon at a time to make a firm loaf.

1. Preheat the oven to 350 degrees. Lightly oil a cookie sheet with sides.

2. In a large bowl, mix all the meatloaf ingredients.

3. Form the meat mixture into a loaf and place on a cookie sheet or similar flat pan with sides. Brush the meatloaf with the hoisin sauce. Sprinkle the top with the crushed corn chips. Bake for 1 hour or until done.

4. Let the loaf sit for 10 minutes. Then slice and serve with salsa or chili sauce.

Southwestern Meatloaf

———•———

Janet Hummel
SOUTH ORANGE, NEW JERSEY

WMHQ Note: From New Jersey comes a loaf that blends salsa, cilantro, and Monterey Jack with jalapeño pepper cheese, proving that you don't have to live in the Southwest to make a meatloaf with a kick.

SERVES 6 to 8

6 ounces Monterey Jack cheese
  with jalapeño pepper, grated
1 cup plain bread crumbs*
2 tablespoons minced cilantro
¾ pound ground beef
½ pound ground pork

½ pound ground veal
2 large eggs, lightly beaten
½ cup salsa, preferably hot
1 teaspoon salt
⅛ teaspoon black pepper
Chopped cilantro for garnish

1. Preheat the oven to 350 degrees. Lightly coat a 9 × 5 × 3-inch loaf pan.

2. In a large bowl, combine all but 1 tablespoon of the cheese with the bread crumbs, cilantro, ground beef, ground pork, and ground veal. Add the eggs, salsa, salt, and black pepper, and mix thoroughly.

3. Place the meat mixture in the prepared pan and sprinkle the remaining tablespoon of cheese over the top.

4. Shape a piece of aluminum foil into an inverted *v* and place over the loaf. Bake for 1 hour or until done. Remove the loaf from the oven. Pour off the excess fat. Let the loaf sit for 10 to 15 minutes. Remove the loaf to a serving platter. Garnish with cilantro.

*If necessary, add more bread crumbs a tablespoon at a time to make a firm loaf.

Mexican Crock-Pot Meatloaf

———————•———————

NANCY CREW

NAPOLEON, OHIO

WMHQ Notes: The sixties are back. Now is the time to take out the Crock-Pot you got for a wedding gift those many years ago. You can make this loaf in the morning, turn on the pot, go to work, pick up your cleaning, mow the back forty, take a shower, and it's ready to serve (and only one pot to clean). Plug in the Crock-Pot before you leave in the morning. I forgot to the first time.

If you don't have a Crock-Pot, use a lightly oiled 9 × 5 × 3-inch loaf pan and bake at 350 degrees for 1 hour or until done.

SERVES 6 to 8

2 pounds ground beef
⅔ cup taco sauce
4 tablespoons packaged taco mix (add more if you'd like a spicier loaf)

2 cups coarsely crushed corn chips*
2 large eggs, lightly beaten
1 cup grated Monterey Jack or cheddar cheese

1. In a large bowl, mix all the ingredients.

2. Shape into a loaf. Place in a Crock-Pot.

3. Cover and cook on low 8 to 10 hours or on high 3½ to 5 hours.

*If necessary, add more chip crumbs a tablespoon at a time to make a firm loaf.

1992 First Place—The Great American Meatloaf National Recipe Contest, Meatloaf Category

Jeff's Mama's Meatloaf

•

Jeff Cahill

ALPHARETTA, GEORGIA

WMHQ Note: This prize-winning loaf has a surprise kick to it. Jeff's recipe includes Jack Daniel's as a unique way to flavor the meatloaf. Jeff worked diligently to achieve the perfect blend of spices and seasonings. It's a loaf we've made again and again.

Serves 6 to 8

3 large celery stalks, with leaves chopped finely
½ large red onion, chopped
1 large green bell pepper (half chopped and other half sliced for garnish)
2 pounds ground beef
¼ lemon
¼ lime
2 shots Jack Daniel's whiskey
2 large eggs, lightly beaten
2 cups ketchup
6 tablespoons Jamaican Pickapeppa or other hot sauce

2 tablespoons Jane's Krazy Mixed Up Salt or other seasoned salt
1 teaspoon minced garlic
1 teaspoon light brown sugar, packed
1 teaspoon yellow prepared mustard
2 teaspoons Mrs. Dash seasoning mix
1 teaspoon black pepper
1 tablespoon salt
3 slices whole wheat bread*

(continued)

---

*If necessary, add more bread a few pieces at a time to make a firm loaf.

1. Preheat the oven to 325 degrees. Lightly oil a 2-quart baking dish.

2. Combine the celery, onion, and ½ green bell pepper with the ground beef in a large mixing bowl.

3. Squeeze the lemon and lime into the mixture, then add the Jack Daniel's.

4. Add the eggs, 2 cups ketchup, and remaining ingredients.

5. Hold the bread briefly under running water and squeeze out the excess water like a sponge. Tear the bread into pieces and add to the meat mixture.

6. Form the mixture into a loaf and place in the prepared baking dish. Keep a 1-inch margin around the meat to allow the grease to collect and be drained off.

7. Spread the remaining ketchup on top of the loaf, garnishing with the sliced peppers.

8. Cook for 1½ hours or until done. Let the loaf sit for 10 minutes before slicing.

Chapter 6

Dinner Party
Meatloaves

*T*he recipes in this chapter are presented for your more formal meatloaf occasions: visiting heads of state, mothers-in-law, top fashion models—whomever you decide to favor with the meatloaves in this chapter, they'll be impressed.

These recipes use the basic idea of meatloaf—meat, binders, herbs, and spices—and include creative additions. If you enjoy cooking and experimenting with new recipes, this is the chapter for you. Have fun!

FEAR OF THE UNKNOWN

I'll admit that when I first looked at some of these recipes in their original form, I kept putting them in the "Test Next Month" file. As next month finally came, those of us at World Meatloaf Headquarters had to overcome our fear of using ingredients we had never used before, or cooking techniques we had never tried. But we learned that most of the things we were nervous to try were actually very easy once we carefully read the recipe and gathered all our ingredients before cooking.

Here are some things we've learned:

1. Read the recipe a few times before you start cooking. All the recipes are broken down into steps. The steps are logical and have been tested by noncooking professionals—us.

2. If you gather all your ingredients before you start, you'll save a few miles of wear and tear on your shoes, roaming around your kitchen or having to run to the store in the middle of cooking. If a recipe calls for a sauce or gravy and you don't want to make it from scratch, *don't!* There are commercial gravies and sauces that will work fine.

3. Do not make a recipe for the first time when you are hosting a dinner party. Use your family and good friends to experiment on if you're not comfortable with a recipe.

Firehouse Meatloaf

●

PETER F. BAZYDLO

SYRACUSE, NEW YORK

"I am one of the cooks on my shift at the firehouse, and I developed this recipe on one of my nights to cook."
—PETER F. BAZYDLO

SERVES 8 to 10

¼ cup olive oil
3 garlic cloves, crushed
1 cup diced sweet onion
⅓ cup diced red bell pepper
⅓ cup diced green bell pepper
1 pound ground beef
½ pound ground pork
¼ pound mild Italian sausage, casing removed
¼ pound hot Italian sausage, casing removed
4 large eggs, lightly beaten
⅔ cup Italian-flavored bread crumbs*
2 tablespoons grated Parmesan cheese

2 tablespoons grated Romano cheese
¼ cup honey barbecue sauce
¼ cup ketchup
1 tablespoon Hellman's Dijonnaise, or ½ tablespoon Dijon mustard mixed with ½ tablespoon mayonnaise
1 tablespoon Italian seasoning
4 drops hot sauce
⅛ teaspoon dried hot red pepper flakes
¼ teaspoon ground cumin
⅛ teaspoon dried marjoram
½ teaspoon dried sage

(*continued*)

*If necessary, add more bread crumbs a tablespoon at a time to make a firm loaf.

1. Preheat the oven to 350 degrees. Lightly oil a broiler pan with slits.

2. In a sauté pan, warm the oil over low heat. Add the garlic, onion, and bell peppers. Cook until tender, about 4 to 5 minutes.

3. In a large bowl, combine the ground beef, ground pork, mild sausage, and hot sausage. Add the sautéed vegetables and mix well.

4. In another bowl, combine the eggs, bread crumbs, Parmesan and Romano cheeses, and remaining ingredients. Add to the meat mixture and mix well.

5. Form into a loaf and place on the lightly oiled broiler pan placed on a roasting pan so the meatloaf will drain. Rub the meatloaf with ice water before baking. Cook for 1¼ hours or until done. Let the loaf sit for 10 minutes before slicing.

Pizza Meatloaf

•

HAZEL E. NUTE
TACOMA, WASHINGTON

WMHQ Note: Why order a pizza to be delivered when you can make your own without hassle? If you like olives on your pizza, you'll love this loaf.

SERVES 8

Meatloaf

1 pound turkey sausage*
1 pound lean ground beef
1 teaspoon celery salt
1 4-ounce can mushrooms,
 including stems and pieces,
 drained
1 teaspoon dried basil
½ teaspoon dried thyme
½ teaspoon dried oregano
4¼ ounces ripe olives,
 chopped

1 medium onion, finely
 chopped
½ teaspoon garlic powder
2 large eggs, lightly beaten
1 green bell pepper, chopped
½ teaspoon white pepper
½ 14-ounce jar pizza or
 spaghetti sauce
½ cup Italian-flavored bread
 crumbs†

Topping

½ 14-ounce jar pizza or
 spaghetti sauce

2¼ ounces ripe olives, sliced
 and drained

1. Preheat the oven to 350 degrees. Lightly oil a large piece of foil and line a 9 × 13-inch metal baking pan with it.

2. In a large bowl, combine the meatloaf ingredients and mix well.

3. Form the meatloaf mixture into a 9 × 5-inch loaf.

4. Top the meatloaf with the remaining half-jar of pizza or spaghetti sauce and the sliced olives.

5. Bake for 1½ hours, or until done. Let the meatloaf sit for 15 minutes before slicing and serving.

---

*Turkey sausage is available in the deli section of most supermarkets. It is a spicy alternative to pork sausage and is lower in fat.
†If necessary, add more bread crumbs a tablespoon at a time to make a firm loaf.

French Fleur-de-Lis Meatloaf Microwave Magic

TILLIE ASTORINO

NORTH ADAMS, MASSACHUSETTS

WMHQ Note: Tillie created this recipe especially for the contest. A cooking contest veteran, she showed up bright and early the day of the cookoff and impressed the judges not only with the taste of this loaf but with her presentation. Tillie cooked her meatloaf in muffin cups and then arranged the individual meatloaves on a serving platter surrounding the Spicy Spinach Salsa. She also cut up carrots, celery, and other vegetables and displayed them on the tray with the meatloaf.

SERVES 6 to 8

Meatloaf

2 pounds ground sirloin
⅓ cup quick oats*
⅓ cup instant dry potato flakes
2 egg whites
½ teaspoon lemon pepper
½ teaspoon salt
½ teaspoon garlic powder
½ teaspoon ground thyme
½ teaspoon ground cumin
½ teaspoon ground cardamom
2 tablespoons chopped black
  olives

2 tablespoons chopped capers
2 tablespoons chopped
  jalapeño pepper
2 tablespoons chopped roasted
  red pepper
½ cup shredded Provolone
  cheese
½ cup ground pistachios
½ cup ground almonds

Spicy Spinach Salsa

6 ounces fresh spinach, stems
  removed
1 jalapeño pepper, stem and
  seeds removed
3 scallions, finely minced
½ cup low-fat yogurt

½ cup ranch dressing
1 tablespoon Dijon honey
  mustard
1 tablespoon mint or red
  pepper jelly

Optional Garnish

Lettuce leaves

Carrots and celery, cut into
  3-inch slices

1. Lightly oil a microwave-safe 6-cup muffin pan. (Or, if you are using an oven, preheat the oven to 350 degrees and prepare a standard 6-cup muffin pan.)

(*continued*)

*If necessary, add more oats a tablespoon at a time to make a firm loaf.

2. Combine all the meatloaf ingredients except the almonds and pistachios. Shape into 6 equal-size balls.

3. Roll the balls in the ground almonds and pistachios.

4. Place each ball in a muffin cup. Microwave on High for 12 to 15 minutes. If you don't have a turntable in your microwave, rotate the muffin pan twice during cooking. (If using a conventional oven, bake the meatloaf muffins for 45 minutes or until done.) Let them cool for 10 minutes before removing from the pan.

5. Meanwhile, in a food processor or blender, process the spinach, jalapeño pepper, and scallions for 2 minutes, until the mixture reaches the consistency of paste. Blend in the yogurt, dressing, mustard, and jelly. Refrigerate for 30 minutes.

6. Remove the meatloaves from the pan. Place them in a circle on a lettuce-lined platter. Serve the dressing in a bowl in the center. Place vegetable crudités around the outer edge of the plate.

Top of the Stove Meatloaf

•————————

CAROL SANDS
LYNN, MASSACHUSETTS

"This is my mother's recipe, Mrs. Joan R. de Langis." —CAROL SANDS

WMHQ Note: The stove-top technique enhances the flavor of the sirloin. The gravy is easy to make and can also be served over a side dish of egg noodles, or with Garlic Mashed Potatoes (page 291). This loaf should be served immediately after cooking. You can also add halved Red Bliss potatoes to the pan for 30 minutes and serve them with your meatloaf.

SERVES 6 to 8

Meatloaf

2 pounds ground sirloin
¼ cup finely chopped onion
1 tablespoon ground allspice
2 large eggs, lightly beaten

¼ teaspoon black pepper
¼ teaspoon salt
1 cup finely crushed saltine
  crackers*

Sauce

1 tablespoon vegetable oil
2 cups water
2 large bay leaves
2 garlic cloves
1 beef bouillon cube
2 tablespoons cornstarch
  mixed with 2 tablespoons
  water

1 4-ounce can mushrooms
  (optional)
¼ teaspoon Gravy Master
  (optional, for color)

(*continued*)

*If necessary, add more cracker crumbs a tablespoon at a time to make a firm loaf.

1. In a large bowl, combine all the meatloaf ingredients. Mix thoroughly. Shape the mixture into a loaf.

2. In a heavy cast-iron 8-quart pot or Dutch oven, heat the oil. Add the meatloaf and sear the meat all around by turning it with 2 spatulas, being careful not to break the loaf's shape.

3. Add the water, bay leaves, bouillon cube, and garlic to the pot. Cover and simmer for about 2 hours. (Check the loaf after 1 hour to see if additional water is needed.)

4. Remove the loaf and cover with foil to keep warm.

5. Pour the broth from the pan through a strainer into a gravy separator to remove the fat. If you don't have a gravy separator, put the liquid in a bowl and refrigerate until you see the fat separate from the gravy. Remove the fat with a spoon.

6. Pour the degreased broth back into the pan and turn the heat to high to bring it to a quick boil. Add the cornstarch and water mixture to the broth and stir to thicken. If using, add the mushrooms and/or Gravy Master to the thickened broth. Serve the loaf hot with vegetables and mashed potatoes.

Good Ol' Boys' Favorite

————•————

BEVERLY A. CASEY
BARRE, VERMONT

WMHQ Note: Meatloaf becomes an omelet in this recipe. You can have a lot of fun being creative with this one. My favorite version of this meatloaf is to skip the tomatoes and substitute bacon which has been parboiled for 3 minutes. You can also experiment with different kinds of cheeses.

SERVES 6

2 tablespoons butter
1 medium onion, chopped
1 green bell pepper, chopped
1 3-ounce can mushrooms, drained
1½ pounds ground beef
½ cup plain bread crumbs*
1 large egg, lightly beaten
½ cup ketchup
2 teaspoons prepared horseradish

1 teaspoon salt
½ teaspoon black pepper
2 tablespoons Worcestershire sauce
1 medium tomato, cut in 6 slices
1½ cups shredded sharp cheddar cheese†

1. Preheat the oven to 350 degrees. Lightly coat a 9 × 13 × 2-inch baking pan with nonstick cooking spray.

(continued)

*If necessary, add more bread crumbs a tablespoon at a time to make a firm loaf.
†We've found that fatty cheeses separate when they are cooked. We substituted a lower fat sharp cheddar cheese when we made it a second time. It held together well and tasted delicious.

2. Melt the butter in the skillet. Add the onion and bell pepper. Cook covered over low heat for 10 minutes or until tender, stirring occasionally. Do not brown. Remove from the heat and add the mushrooms.

3. In a separate bowl, combine the ground beef with the bread crumbs, egg, ketchup, horseradish, salt, pepper, and Worcestershire sauce.

4. Turn the mixture onto wax paper and flatten with your hands into a circle 12 inches in diameter.

5. Spread the sautéed vegetables from step 1 on the left half of the meatloaf circle. Top with 3 slices of tomato and sprinkle with half the shredded cheddar cheese.

6. Fold the right half of the meatloaf circle over the filling and seal the edges well to form a crescent.

7. Transfer the meatloaf to the baking pan and bake for 40 to 45 minutes, or until done.

8. Remove and top the crescent loaf with the remaining slices of tomato and sprinkle with the remaining cheese.

9. Return to the oven for a couple of minutes to melt the cheese. Remove and serve hot. Or broil the crescent loaf to melt the cheese. Watch it carefully!

Caribbean Meatloaf with Spanish Sauce

•

LINDA GIZIENSKI
COVENTRY, RHODE ISLAND

"This is a recipe that I developed while living in Puerto Rico a few years ago. On very short notice, my husband informed me that he was bringing guests home for dinner that evening. I quickly looked in the refrigerator to see what I could prepare and found that I was very low on some of the basic essentials.

"I quickly began preparing an old family meatloaf recipe that I modified over the years by adding quick oats, Ritz crackers, and bacon. I wanted to add a zesty topping to provide a different taste and decided to add the Spanish Sauce recipe that I had developed earlier. The meal was a success with the Caribbean Meatloaf with Spanish Sauce getting rave reviews." —LINDA GIZIENSKI

SERVES 6

Spanish Sauce

3 medium onions, chopped
1 green bell pepper, chopped
2 celery stalks, diced
¼ teaspoon salt
½ teaspoon black pepper
3 cups water or enough to cover vegetables in saucepan

1 8-ounce can tomatoes with juice
½ teaspoon red pepper flakes
1½ tablespoons cornstarch mixed with 1½ tablespoons water

(continued)

Meatloaf

1½ pounds lean ground beef
¼ cup chopped onion
1 cup quick oats*
⅓ cup milk

1 large egg, lightly beaten
¼ teaspoon salt
½ teaspoon pepper
1 cup crushed Ritz crackers

Topping

½ cup tomato sauce

4 strips bacon, uncooked

1. Preheat the oven to 350 degrees. Lightly oil a 9 × 5 × 3-inch loaf pan.
2. In a large saucepan, combine the onions, green pepper, celery, salt, and black pepper. Add water and cook over medium-high heat.
3. When the vegetable mixture starts to boil, add the juice from the can of tomatoes and the red pepper flakes. Reserve the tomatoes for later use. Reduce the heat, cover the pan, and cook for 20 minutes over medium heat.
4. After 20 minutes, reduce the heat to low and remove the cover.
5. Add the cornstarch and water mixture to thicken the vegetable mixture. Add the tomatoes and simmer over low heat for 10 minutes while gently stirring. Reheat the sauce when ready to serve.
6. In a large bowl, combine the ground beef, onion, oats, milk, egg, salt, and black pepper.
7. Shape the mixture into a loaf and roll in crushed crackers until completely covered.
8. Place the loaf in the prepared pan and top with the tomato sauce and strips of bacon.
9. Bake for 1¼ hours or until done. Using 2 spatulas, remove the meatloaf from the pan and place on a serving platter. Let the loaf sit for 10 minutes before serving. Slice the meatloaf and spoon the sauce over each serving.

*If necessary, add more oats a tablespoon at a time to make a firm loaf.

Lisa's Famous Super Meatloaf

•

JONI DIAMOND-SILVERS
GLOUCESTER, VIRGINIA

"This is a recipe that my daughter originally made up when she was fourteen years old. She loved to cook and took over the responsibility of preparing the meals for her sisters and me. She did this creatively and lovingly, so I am dedicating this recipe to her." —JONI DIAMOND-SILVERS

SERVES 10 to 12

Meatloaf

2 pounds ground beef
2 pounds ground veal
2 pounds ground pork
¾ cup Italian-flavored bread crumbs*
2 large eggs, lightly beaten
¼ cup finely chopped onion
2 tablespoons finely chopped celery
¼ cup milk

¼ cup ketchup
¼ teaspoon poultry seasoning
¼ teaspoon ground sage
¼ teaspoon black pepper
¼ teaspoon dry mustard
1 teaspoon salt
1 cup water
2 tablespoons plus ⅛ teaspoon Worcestershire sauce

Topping

½ cup ketchup
5 bacon strips, uncooked

2 to 3 tablespoons Italian-flavored bread crumbs

(*continued*)

*If necessary, add more bread crumbs a tablespoon at a time to make a firm loaf.

1. Preheat the oven to 350 degrees. Lightly oil a 9 × 13-inch roasting pan.

2. In a large bowl, combine all the meatloaf ingredients except the water and ⅛ teaspoon Worcestershire sauce. Form the meat mixture into a loaf.

3. Place the loaf into the prepared pan, allowing 1½ inches on all sides. Then pour enough water around the loaf for it to come up ¼ inch around the meatloaf. Add ⅛ teaspoon Worcestershire sauce to the water.

4. Cover the top of the loaf with the ketchup and the bacon. Sprinkle with the bread crumbs.

5. Bake uncovered for 1½ to 2 hours, or until done. Baste the loaf with the liquid at least twice while cooking. Let the loaf sit for 15 minutes before serving.

Texas Inside-Out Meatloaf

JIM POWELL
HOUSTON, TEXAS

"Through the years, this recipe has been handed down in my family. It was created by my grandmother." —JIM POWELL

WMHQ Note: Rolling the meatloaf in cracker crumbs gives the loaf a crunchy texture. It also works well with crumbled Cheez-Its or Ritz crackers.

SERVES 8 to 10

2 pounds lean ground beef
1 pound ground pork
½ large green bell pepper, diced
1 large celery stalk, diced
1 medium onion, grated
3 large eggs, lightly beaten
1 cup ketchup

1 10¾-ounce can cream of mushroom soup
2 teaspoons celery seed
2 cups tomato juice
⅛ teaspoon salt
⅛ teaspoon black pepper
20 to 30 saltine crackers, crumbled

1. Preheat the oven to 350 degrees. Lightly oil a 9 × 13 × 2-inch roasting pan.

2. In a large bowl, combine all the ingredients except the cracker crumbs. Mix well.

3. Form the meat mixture into a loaf.

4. Spread the cracker crumbs on a large piece of wax paper. Carefully roll the loaf in the cracker crumbs. Cover the loaf completely with the crumbs.

5. Place the loaf in the prepared pan. Bake the meatloaf for 1½ to 2 hours, or until done. Drain off all accumulated juices before serving. Let the loaf sit for 10 minutes before slicing.

Red, White, and Blue-Cheese Meatloaf

TERRIE DUNKELBERGER
SOUTHPORT, CONNECTICUT

WMHQ Note: This is a real crowd pleaser because it is well-seasoned and creative with the blue cheese and capers. Serve it when a favorite client, your boss, or a bill collector comes to dinner. (Although why anyone would be entertaining a bill collector is beyond me.) Check first to make sure your guests like blue cheese.

SERVES 8

Meatloaf

2½ pounds ground sirloin
1 cup crushed croutons (herb-garlic flavored preferred)*
2 large eggs, lightly beaten
2 tablespoons dried oregano
1 tablespoon dried basil
1 tablespoon black pepper
4 tablespoons Worcestershire sauce
1 tablespoon grainy Dijon or Pommeroy mustard
½ cup ketchup

½ cup sun-dried tomatoes packed in oil, drained, 1 tablespoon of the oil reserved
1 cup sliced scallions (with green part)
5 garlic cloves, minced
½ red bell pepper, diced
1 pound blue cheese, crumbled
2 teaspoons drained capers
3 tablespoons chopped fresh parsley

*If necessary, add more crushed croutons a tablespoon at a time to make a firm loaf.

Glaze

¼ cup ketchup

1. Preheat the oven to 350 degrees. Lightly oil a large piece of aluminum foil and line a 10 × 13-inch roasting pan.

2. In a large bowl, combine the sirloin, croutons, eggs, oregano, basil, black pepper, Worcestershire sauce, mustard, and ketchup. Mix well.

3. In a large saucepan, heat the reserved tablespoon of sun-dried tomato oil and add the scallions, garlic, red pepper, and sun-dried tomatoes. Sauté over high heat until scallions are translucent, about 3 minutes.

4. Let the mixture cool and drain any excess oil and liquid. Add to the meat mixture.

5. In a small bowl, combine the blue cheese, capers, and parsley, and set aside.

6. Divide the meat mixture into 2 equal portions and form each into identical size rectangles. Place one rectangle in the prepared pan.

7. Hollow out a depression 1 inch in from all sides. Place the blue cheese mixture in the depression. Place the other sirloin rectangle on top, and seal all the sides.

8. Glaze the top of the loaf with the ketchup.

9. Bake for 1 hour and 15 minutes, or until done. Let it sit for 15 minutes before serving.

Meatloaf with Three Cheeses

———————•———————

CHARLOTTE RODENFELS

COLUMBUS, OHIO

WMHQ Note: This is a loaf for cheese lovers. With Parmesan, mozzarella, and Gruyère (or Swiss), you've got a great combination of cheeses that won't mask the other flavors in the loaf.
This recipe makes two loaves.

SERVES 8 to 10

3 tablespoons plain bread crumbs plus enough to coat 2 buttered loaf pans
3 pounds ground beef
1 large onion, chopped
1 garlic clove, minced
2 cups fresh spinach leaves, rinsed, thoroughly dried, and chopped
½ cup grated Parmesan cheese
3 tablespoons finely chopped fresh parsley

3 large eggs, lightly beaten
1 teaspoon salt
⅛ teaspoon black pepper
4 slices French or Italian bread*
¼ cup milk
4 ounces mozzarella cheese, cubed
4 ounces Gruyère or Swiss cheese, cubed
2 tablespoons butter

*If necessary, add more soaked bread a tablespoon at a time to make a firm loaf.

1. Preheat the oven to 350 degrees. Grease two 9 × 5 × 3-inch loaf pans with butter. Sprinkle pan with some of the bread crumbs, making sure the bottom and sides are coated. Shake out excess bread crumbs.

2. In a large bowl, combine the meat, onion, garlic, spinach, Parmesan cheese, parsley, eggs, salt, and pepper. Mix well.

3. In a separate bowl, soak the bread in the milk for 5 minutes. Drain and squeeze dry and mix into the meat mixture.

4. Divide the meat mixture into 6 portions. Pat one-sixth of the meat mixture into the bottom of each prepared pan. Be sure the meat touches the sides of the pans. Sprinkle half the mozzarella on top of each loaf.

5. Add another sixth of the meat mixture to each pan and cover with half the Gruyère or Swiss for each loaf.

6. Add the remaining meat mixture, pressing it to the edges of the pans. Sprinkle with remaining bread crumbs and dot each meatloaf with the butter.

7. Bake for 45 minutes to 1 hour or until done. Let the loaves sit for 10 minutes before removing them to a serving platter.

Aloha Meatloaf

—————•—————

Bonnie S. Baumgardner

Sylva, North Carolina

WMHQ Note: One of the meatloaf analysts at World Meatloaf Headquarters suggests serving the warm Aloha Sauce over ice cream. Always trying to be on the cutting edge in the culinary world, we tried it. Fantastic! We also promoted him to Head Meatloaf Analyst. Now there's an honor his family is proud of.

Serves 6

Meatloaf

1 pound ground sirloin
1 pound ground veal
1 cup crushed unsalted saltine
  crackers*
½ cup sour cream
2 large eggs, well beaten
1 teaspoon salt
½ teaspoon black pepper

1 medium onion, chopped
1 garlic clove, minced
1 small red bell pepper,
  chopped
¼ cup chopped olives stuffed
  with pimiento
¼ cup cranberry sauce
  (optional)

Aloha Sauce

1 15¼-ounce can crushed
  pineapple
1 tablespoon soy sauce
1 tablespoon steak sauce
½ cup applesauce

¼ teaspoon ground cinnamon
⅓ cup chopped pecans
⅓ cup chopped golden raisins
2 tablespoons cornstarch
2 tablespoons water

*If necessary, add more cracker crumbs a tablespoon at a time to make a firm loaf.

Optional Garnish

Fresh parsley
Red bell pepper, cut into rings

Yellow bell pepper, cut into
rings

1. Preheat the oven to 350 degrees. Lightly oil a 9 × 5 × 3-inch loaf pan.

2. In a large bowl, combine the meatloaf ingredients and mix well.

3. Press the meatloaf mixture into the prepared pan.

4. Make criss-cross marks with a knife or spatula on the top of the loaf.

5. Bake for 1 hour, or until done.

6. In a medium saucepan, mix the pineapple, soy sauce, steak sauce, applesauce, cinnamon, pecans, and raisins.

7. In a small bowl, add the cornstarch and water and stir well. Add the cornstarch and water to the pineapple mixture and cook, stirring constantly, until it begins to boil. Boil the mixture for 3 minutes or until it thickens. Set aside.

8. When the meatloaf is done, let it sit for 10 minutes. Remove the loaf to a serving platter. Garnish with parsley and red and yellow pepper rings. When ready to serve, slice the meatloaf, reheat the pineapple sauce, and serve over the meatloaf.

Meatloaf Cormak

———•———

JOHN F. MCCORMACK, JR.
WAKEFIELD, MASSACHUSETTS

WMHQ Note: John has really done a great job here. Not only is the meat-loaf delicious but the sauce is brilliant! Don't let the long ingredients list intimidate you. Once you have all of your ingredients together, it's simple to assemble.

SERVES 8

Meatloaf

2½ pounds ground sirloin or
  lean ground beef
2 extra-large eggs, lightly
  beaten
1 green bell pepper, diced
2 tablespoons grated Parmesan
  or Romano cheese
1 large onion, diced
2 garlic cloves, finely chopped
1 celery stalk, diced
2 slices day-old white bread,
  broken into small pieces
1 tablespoon dried oregano

2 tablespoons poultry
  seasoning
⅛ teaspoon salt
⅛ teaspoon black pepper
¼ cup Italian-flavored bread
  crumbs*
8 drops hot sauce
2 tablespoons Worcestershire
  sauce
Juice of ½ lemon
¼ cup milk
2 tablespoons red wine
  vinegar

*If necessary, add more bread crumbs a tablespoon at a time to make a firm loaf.

Topping

2 tablespoons ketchup   2 strips bacon, uncooked

Sauce

½ green bell pepper, cut into
  strips
¼ teaspoon dried oregano
1 celery stalk, diced
1 medium onion, cut into rings
⅛ teaspoon sugar

¼ teaspoon Worcestershire
  sauce
⅛ teaspoon salt
⅛ teaspoon black pepper
1 16-ounce can tomato sauce

1. Preheat the oven to 350 degrees. Lightly oil a 9 × 5 × 3-inch loaf pan.

2. In a large bowl, combine the meatloaf ingredients and mix well.

3. Place the meatloaf mixture into the prepared loaf pan.

4. Coat the top of the loaf with the ketchup and place the bacon strips on top.

5. Bake for 1½ to 2 hours uncovered, or until done. Pour off the excess drippings occasionally while cooking. Let the loaf sit for 10 to 15 minutes, then remove the loaf from the pan.

6. While the meatloaf is cooking, place the sauce ingredients in a medium saucepan and simmer over low heat for 30 minutes.

7. Slice the meatloaf and pour a small amount of the sauce on each slice. Place the remaining sauce in a gravy boat to accompany the meatloaf.

Beef, Brew, 'n Pretzel Ring

●

SHIRLEY DeSANTIS

EAST WINDSOR, NEW JERSEY

WMHQ Note: This is a fun loaf! Combining pretzels and beer can only be called genius. Shirley must have had fun testing this recipe. We sure did. For an impressive presentation, Shirley recommends filling the ring with pretzels and serving it with your favorite beer.

SERVES 8 to 10

Meatloaf

2½ pounds ground beef
⅔ cup beer
1 large egg, lightly beaten
1½ cups crushed salted
   pretzels*
1 medium onion, chopped

2 tablespoons spicy brown
   mustard
½ teaspoon black pepper
½ teaspoon minced garlic
3 tablespoons steak sauce

Glaze

½ cup ketchup
⅓ cup beer

1 tablespoon spicy brown
   mustard

---

*Place the pretzels in a plastic bag and then hit hard with anything handy. It's a great stress reliever. If necessary, add more pretzel crumbs a tablespoon at a time to make a firm loaf.

Topping

⅔ cup shredded hot pepper
  cheese

Garnish

2 tablespoons chopped fresh   Pretzels
  parsley

1. Preheat the oven to 350 degrees. Line a 6-cup ring mold with plastic wrap, or shape the loaf into a ring shape. Line a baking sheet with sides with aluminum foil.

2. In a large bowl, combine the meatloaf ingredients.

3. Pack the mixture into the prepared mold. Refrigerate for 30 minutes so the meatloaf will easily come out of the mold.

4. Coat a baking or cooling rack with nonstick cooking spray. Place the rack on the lined cookie sheet.

5. Unmold the beef ring onto the rack.

6. Bake uncovered for 50 minutes.

7. In a small bowl combine the ketchup, beer, and mustard. Mix well.

8. After 50 minutes, remove the beef ring from the oven and drizzle the glaze on top.

9. Return the beef ring to the oven for 10 to 15 minutes.

10. Remove the beef ring and sprinkle the shredded hot pepper cheese on the loaf. Return it to the oven until the cheese melts (about 5 minutes).

11. Let the loaf sit for 10 minutes. Remove it to a serving plate and garnish with the parsley and pretzels.

Monterey Magic Meatloaf with Magic Sauce

MARY-ALICE RODES
DORAVILLE, GEORGIA

"I'm a retired airline employee. I'm not Spanish or Mexican, I just like Mexican food very much. I am always trying to find a way to fix it at home."

—MARY-ALICE RODES

SERVES 4 to 6

Meatloaf

1 pound ground beef
5 pieces hickory-smoked
    bacon, fried and crumbled
¼ teaspoon black pepper
¼ teaspoon salt
¼ teaspoon sugar
½ cup canned niblet corn
1 large egg, lightly beaten
¼ cup chopped green bell
    pepper

¼ cup chopped onion
1 tablespoon diced canned
    green chilies
¼ cup skim milk
1 teaspoon chili powder
1 cup shredded Monterey Jack
    cheese

Magic Sauce

1 teaspoon cornstarch
1 cup water
2 tablespoons tomato paste
¼ teaspoon salt
1 tablespoon canned niblet
   corn

1 tablespoon chopped canned
   green chilies
½ cup shredded Monterey
   Jack cheese

1. Preheat the oven to 350 degrees. Lightly oil a piece of aluminum foil and line a 9 × 5 × 3-inch loaf pan with it.

2. In a large bowl, combine the meatloaf ingredients. Mix well.

3. Press the meatloaf mixture in the prepared pan and bake for 1 hour or until done.

4. In a small bowl mix the cornstarch and the water. In a small saucepan over medium heat, warm the tomato paste. Add the cornstarch and water mixture, stirring constantly. Add the salt, corn, and chilies and mix well. Stir in the cheese until it melts.

5. When the meatloaf is done, drain the grease and let it sit for 10 minutes. Turn the meatloaf out onto a serving dish, pour the sauce over the meatloaf, and serve.

Meatloaf Pie

•

Emily S. Membrino
WATERBURY, CONNECTICUT

WMHQ Note: Instead of using ham, you could use prosciutto or increase the amount of raisins.

When we first saw this recipe, we didn't see how it would work. But the judges were surprised how great it tasted! This is a loaf that will impress your guests when you slice it at the table. And it's easy to put together.

Serves 6 to 8

Meatloaf

1½ pounds ground beef
2 teaspoons salt
3 large eggs, lightly beaten
1 teaspoon black pepper

⅔ cup plain bread crumbs*
1½ teaspoons parsley flakes
2½ tablespoons grated
 Parmesan cheese

---

*If necessary, add more bread crumbs a tablespoon at a time to make a firm loaf.

Filling

3 slices Swiss cheese
3 slices cooked ham
1 hard-boiled egg, sliced

5 strips bacon, cooked
2½ tablespoons raisins
4 slices Muenster cheese

Garnish

4 black olives, sliced

4 green olives, sliced

1. Preheat the oven to 375 degrees. Coat the bottom of a 10-inch glass or ceramic deep-dish pie plate with nonstick cooking spray.

2. In a large bowl, mix the meatloaf ingredients.

3. Press two-thirds of the meatloaf mixture into the pie plate and up the sides as well.

4. Layer the filling ingredients on top of the meatloaf in the order given.

5. Top with the remaining meatloaf mixture.

6. Garnish the top of the loaf with the olive rings.

7. Bake, covered with aluminum foil, for 20 minutes. Remove the foil and continue baking for 25 minutes or until the top browns.

Sweet Confetti Meatloaf

———————•———————

DOROTHY S. KROKO

SANTA ANA, CALIFORNIA

"Cooking time and temperature are my solutions to preparing dinner so that I can be at the office in the afternoon and return to a ready-in-the-oven meal. On recipe test day, I turned the oven off at 2:15 P.M. and removed the meatloaf from the oven at 5:30 P.M."   —DOROTHY KROKO

WMHQ Note: All the vegetables are finely chopped in a food processor, or you can chop them finely by hand.

SERVES 6 to 8

Meatloaf

1 pound ground sirloin or very
  lean ground beef
1 pound ground turkey
1 teaspoon salt
1 large egg plus 2 egg whites
¾ cup crumbled saltine
  crackers*
¾ cup quick oats
1¼ cups skim milk
¼ cup chopped fresh Italian
  parsley
½ teaspoon black pepper
1 teaspoon ancho chili powder
  or other New Mexico–style
  mild chili powder
¾ cup chopped mushrooms
1 teaspoon vegetable oil

1 small onion
1 large sweet potato
3 medium zucchini
1 red bell pepper
1 4-ounce can mild green
  chilies, chopped
1 garlic clove, minced
½ cup tomato sauce
3 tablespoons chopped fresh
  oregano or 1 tablespoon
  dried
3 tablespoons chopped fresh
  thyme, or 1 tablespoon dried
3 tablespoons chopped fresh
  basil leaves, or 1 tablespoon
  dried

*If necessary, add more cracker crumbs a tablespoon at a time to make a firm loaf.

Topping

3 tablespoons orange juice   ½ cup commercial barbecue
                                  sauce

1. Preheat the oven to 475 degrees. Lightly oil two 9 × 5 × 3-inch
loaf pans.

2. In a large stainless-steel bowl, blend the meats, salt, whole egg,
and egg whites with a table fork (to keep mixture airy and loose).
Do all additional stirring and mixing with a fork. Stir in cracker
crumbs, oats, milk, parsley, black pepper, and chili powder.

3. In a medium skillet, sauté the mushrooms in the vegetable oil
for 2 minutes.

4. In a food processor, finely chop the onion, sweet potato, zucchini, and red pepper. The mixture should look like confetti.

5. Partly fold the mushrooms, chopped vegetables, green chilies,
and garlic into the meat mixture. Add the tomato sauce, oregano,
thyme, and basil and blend thoroughly.

6. In a small bowl, mix the topping ingredients and set aside.

7. Divide the loaf mixture in half and place in the prepared loaf
pans. Spread half the topping on each loaf. Bake for 30 minutes.

8. Turn off the oven and allow the loaves to bake in the dissipating
heat of the oven for at least 2½ hours. The juices will be absorbed,
the vegetable pieces tender, and the loaf ready to serve.

1991 FINALIST—THE GREAT AMERICAN MEATLOAF CONTEST, NORTHEAST REGIONAL COOKOFF

Meatloaf Wellington

•

HARRIET MCCARTER
MADISON, NEW JERSEY

"As someone who loves to cook and likes to experiment, this recipe is the result of mixing and matching various pieces of other dishes I have made over the years. Fortunately, I have a husband who readily volunteers to sample the many attempts it takes to perfect my creations, generally with happy results."

—HARRIET MCCARTER

WMHQ Note: Harriet took a basic meatloaf and dressed it up. Wrapping a meatloaf in pastry is not only delicious but easy to do. This looks great when you slice it at the table.

Meatloaf

2 packages refrigerated ready-
to-use pie crust dough (for
double-crust pies)
1 pound lean ground beef
½ pound ground veal
½ pound lean ground pork
1 small onion, grated
2 large eggs, lightly beaten
¾ cup quick oats*

¾ cup ketchup
¼ cup Worcestershire sauce
1 teaspoon salt
1 teaspoon black pepper
1 teaspoon dried oregano
⅛ teaspoon hot sauce
1 large onion, diced
1 tablespoon vegetable oil

Glaze

1 large egg, lightly beaten

1. Preheat the oven to 350 degrees. Lightly butter all sides of a 9 ×
5 × 3-inch loaf pan. Butter a piece of heavy-duty aluminum foil
and line the bottom and long sides of the pan, extending the foil 2
inches beyond both edges of the loaf pan to serve as handles when
removing the loaf.

2. Unfold the pie crust dough and reshape as needed to cut a 9 ×
13-inch piece for the bottom and long sides, a 10 × 6-inch piece for
the top, and two 4 × 6-inch pieces for the short sides. Line the
prepared pan with the pastry, starting with the largest piece and
adding the short sides, overlapping the edges and moistening with
water to seal.

3. In a large bowl, combine all the ingredients except the diced
onion and oil.

(continued)

---

*If necessary, add more oats a tablespoon at a time to make a firm loaf.

4. In a small skillet, sauté the diced onion in the oil until translucent, about 3 minutes, and then add to the meat mixture. Blend all the ingredients thoroughly.

5. Press the meat mixture into the pastry-lined pan, being careful not to damage the crust and mounding the meat slightly down the middle. Moisten the overhanging edges of pastry with water and add the pastry top, crimping the edges decoratively to seal it.

6. Prick the top of the loaf with a fork in several places to allow the steam to escape, and then brush the entire surface with the beaten egg. (Any leftover pastry scraps can be cut into decorative shapes, placed on the top of the loaf, and glazed.)

7. Bake for 1 to 1¼ hours, covering the top loosely with foil if the pastry begins to brown too quickly.

8. After removing the loaf from the oven, allow it to cool for 20 minutes. Run a knife along the short ends to loosen it from the pan, and grasping the foil handles, lift it out of the pan onto a serving dish, sliding it off the foil in the process.

Barcelona Meatloaf

●

MARSHALL STOWELL

NAPLES, FLORIDA

WMHQ Note: The Barcelona Sauce is versatile. We've used the extra sauce to serve on pasta the next day. We've also crumbled leftover meatloaf and bacon over spaghetti and then topped it with the sauce.

SERVES 6

Meatloaf

2 pounds ground beef
½ pound ground pork
¼ cup chopped onion
1 garlic clove, crushed
¼ cup chopped cilantro
¼ cup milk

½ cup plain bread crumbs*
2 large eggs, lightly beaten
1 tablespoon seasoned salt
1 tablespoon black pepper
3 tablespoons hot sauce
1 tablespoon Italian seasoning

Barcelona Sauce

6 tablespoons olive oil
2 garlic cloves, crushed
1 cup chopped onion
¼ cup chopped cilantro
1 teaspoon black pepper

2 teaspoons hot sauce
1 teaspoon seasoned salt
1 8-ounce can tomato sauce
1 8-ounce can stewed tomatoes
1 cup dry red wine

1. Preheat the oven to 350 degrees. Lightly oil a 9 × 5 × 3-inch loaf pan.

2. In a large bowl, combine the meatloaf ingredients and mix well.

3. Place the meatloaf mixture in the prepared pan. Bake for 1 hour or until done. Let the loaf sit for 10 minutes before slicing.

4. In a large skillet, heat the olive oil. Sauté the garlic and onion for 4 minutes. Place the remaining sauce ingredients in the frying pan and simmer over medium heat for 20 minutes.

5. Top each slice of meatloaf with the sauce and serve extra sauce on the side.

*If necessary, add more bread crumbs a tablespoon at a time to make a firm loaf.

Stuffed Meatloaf with Gingered Pineapple Rum Sauce

―――――――●―――――――

HELEN S. GATELY

CUMBERLAND, RHODE ISLAND

WMHQ Note: The Gingered Pineapple Rum Sauce in this recipe is fantastic! We double it and use it to top hamburgers and other meats.

SERVES 6 to 8

Meatloaf

1½ cups soft fresh bread
    crumbs*
⅓ cup milk
2 large eggs, lightly beaten
¼ cup finely minced scallions

2 teaspoons ground ginger
1 garlic clove, finely minced
1 pound ground beef
1 pound ground veal

Filling

1½ cups cooked rice
½ 8-ounce can crushed
    pineapple, drained and juice
    reserved

¼ cup chopped walnuts

*If necessary, add more bread crumbs a tablespoon at a time to make a firm loaf.

Gingered Pineapple Rum Sauce

½ cup orange juice
2 tablespoons lime juice
3 tablespoons honey
½ teaspoon ground ginger

½ 8-ounce can crushed
  pineapple, drained and juice
  reserved
1 tablespoon cornstarch mixed
  with 1 tablespoon water
2 tablespoons dark rum

1. Preheat the oven to 350 degrees. Line a 9 × 5 × 3-inch loaf pan with plastic. Lightly oil a 9 × 13 × 2-inch baking pan.

2. In a large bowl, combine the bread crumbs and milk and let it sit until the milk is absorbed.

3. Add the eggs, scallions, ginger, and garlic. Mix in the beef and veal, and combine thoroughly.

4. Take three-fourths of the meat mixture and place in the plastic-lined 9 × 5 × 3-inch loaf pan. Make a deep depression in the loaf, pressing the meatloaf mixture up the sides of the pan. The depression in the meatloaf should be deep enough to hold the filling.

5. Mix the rice with the crushed pineapple and walnuts.

6. Pack the filling into the depression of the meatloaf mixture.

7. Cover the filled loaf with the remaining meat mixture and refrigerate for 30 minutes.

8. Unmold the chilled loaf into the prepared 9 × 13 × 2-inch baking pan.

9. Remove the plastic wrap. Bake for 1 hour and 15 minutes, or until done. Let it sit for 10 minutes and remove to a serving platter.

10. In a small saucepan over medium-high heat, combine the reserved pineapple juice, orange juice, lime juice, honey, ginger, and pineapple. Bring to a boil, lower the heat, and simmer for 5 minutes.

(continued)

11. Add the cornstarch and water mixture to the sauce and simmer until slightly thickened, stirring occasionally. Remove from the heat and add the rum.

12. Pour some of the sauce on top of the loaf. Serve the remaining sauce in a gravy boat.

Fruitful Surprise Meatloaf

●

DORIS EBERHARDT
CINCINNATI, OHIO

"This is an old family meatloaf recipe with a new twist that I added. The fruit filling makes an interesting addition to a time-honored meatloaf meal."

—DORIS EBERHARDT

WMHQ Note: I learned a dreaded secret about my mother when we tested this recipe. As we shopped for the ingredients, I picked up the pears needed for the filling. Then it hit me: We never had pears in our house growing up. I called my mother to find out why. Did she have a bad experience with them as a child? Was she forced to pick pears in a labor camp? No, she assured me . . . she just didn't like them. I wonder what else she never told me?

S E R V E S 6 t o 8

Meatloaf

1 pound ground lean beef
½ pound ground veal
½ pound ground pork
1 large egg, lightly beaten
2 slices stale white bread*
1 medium Vidalia or other
   sweet onion, finely chopped
1 large carrot
3 tablespoons cooked rice
¼ cup hot ketchup or regular
   ketchup with a few drops of
   hot sauce to taste

1 teaspoon salt
½ teaspoon black pepper
½ teaspoon paprika
¼ teaspoon ground allspice
¼ teaspoon dried sage
1 tablespoon parsley flakes
1 tablespoon Worcestershire
   sauce

Filling

½ cup peeled and finely
   chopped pear
½ cup peeled and diced
   tomato
¼ cup raisins

¼ cup chopped pecans
½ teaspoon crumbled dried
   tarragon
1 tablespoon lemon juice

Topping

2 tablespoons hot ketchup or
   regular ketchup with a few
   drops of hot sauce to taste

2 strips bacon, uncooked

(*continued*)

*If necessary, add more bread a few pieces at a time to make a firm loaf.

1. Preheat the oven to 350 degrees. Lightly oil a 9 × 5 × 3-inch loaf pan.

2. In a large bowl, combine the ground beef, ground veal, ground pork, and egg. Mix well.

3. Run water over the bread slices. Squeeze out the excess moisture and tear into small pieces.

4. In a food processor, mince the onion and carrot or dice finely with a knife.

5. To the meat mixture add the rice, bread, vegetables, ketchup, salt, pepper, paprika, allspice, sage, parsley, and Worcestershire sauce. Mix well.

6. Place half the meat mixture in the prepared pan. Form a depression in the meatloaf to hold the fruit mixture.

7. In a medium bowl, combine the filling ingredients and mix well.

8. Place the filling mixture in the meatloaf depression. Cover with the remaining meat mixture and press together at the edges.

9. Bake the loaf for 1 hour. Remove from the oven and spread the 2 tablespoons ketchup over the top and lay the bacon strips over the loaf.

10. Return the loaf to the oven and cook another 15 minutes or until the bacon is crisp but not overdone. Remove from the oven and let it sit for 10 minutes. Slice and serve.

Meatloaf with Pesto and Tomato Sauce

●

Elyse Harold
CLEARWATER, FLORIDA

WMHQ Note: Pesto is one of those foods that smell as good as they taste. We doubled the tomato sauce in this recipe and left it in the refrigerator for a few days, and the flavors blended well. If you're short on time, you can substitute a commercial tomato sauce.

Serves 6 to 8

Meatloaf

1 pound ground beef
1 pound ground veal
½ teaspoon salt
2 large eggs, lightly beaten
⅓ cup plain bread crumbs*

¼ cup grated Parmesan cheese
2 teaspoons dry mustard
¼ teaspoon dried basil
1 teaspoon black pepper

Pesto

1 tablespoon olive oil
½ medium onion, chopped
2 garlic cloves, minced

1¾ cups chopped fresh basil
  leaves
¼ cup pine nuts

(continued)

---

*If necessary, add more bread crumbs a tablespoon at a time to make a firm loaf.

Tomato Sauce

2 garlic cloves, minced
2 scallions, minced
2 tablespoons olive oil
1 16-ounce can tomatoes in
    juice, chopped
2 tablespoons tomato paste
½ cup fresh or canned chicken
    broth

¼ cup dry white wine
1 bay leaf
10 fresh basil leaves, chopped
2 sprigs parsley, chopped
½ teaspoon salt
¼ teaspoon black pepper

Filling

6 thin slices prosciutto

Garnish

4 fresh basil leaves, chopped

1. Preheat the oven to 375 degrees. Lightly coat a 9 × 5 × 3-inch loaf pan with nonstick cooking spray.

2. In a large bowl, combine the meatloaf ingredients. Mix well and set aside.

3. Heat the olive oil in a medium skillet. Add the onion, garlic, and basil, stirring until tender.

4. Add the pine nuts and sauté a few minutes. Remove the pan from the heat and set aside.

5. In a large skillet, sauté the garlic and scallions in olive oil until translucent, about 3 minutes. Add the tomatoes and juice and bring to a boil.

6. Add the tomato paste, chicken broth, wine, bay leaf, basil, parsley, salt, and pepper. Bring to a boil again. Reduce heat to medium and cook for 10 to 12 minutes or until the sauce has thickened.

7. Discard the bay leaf and put the mixture in a food processor or blender. Blend to a fine puree.

8. Place half the meat mixture in the pan. Spread the pesto on top of the meat, then arrange the prosciutto slices.

9. Put the other half of the meat mixture on top of the prosciutto. Bake for 1 hour or until done. Let the loaf sit for 10 minutes before removing it from the pan.

10. Remove the meatloaf to a serving platter.

11. To serve, spread the tomato sauce on each plate, then place slices of meatloaf on top of the tomato sauce. Garnish with fresh basil and serve.

1991 THIRD PLACE—THE GREAT AMERICAN MEATLOAF CONTEST, NORTHEAST REGIONAL COOKOFF

New England Pork and Veal Meatloaf

LOUIS LEONCINI

TRUMBULL, CONNECTICUT

WMHQ Note: This is truly a creative meatloaf! This prize-winning loaf has a pork tenderloin in the middle.

SERVES 6 to 8

¾ pound pork tenderloin, trimmed of fat

2 teaspoons black pepper

3 tablespoons corn oil

1 cup diced onion

¾ cup diced red bell pepper

4 ounces shiitake mushrooms, stems removed and julienned

½ cup dry white wine

2 teaspoons chopped fresh rosemary

⅛ teaspoon dried thyme

⅛ teaspoon dried marjoram

¼ teaspoon ground allspice

1½ pounds ground pork

1¼ pounds ground veal

1 slice prosciutto (⅜ inch thick), diced

2 slices white bread,* crumbled

¼ teaspoon garlic powder

4 tablespoons hot and spicy barbecue sauce

2 large eggs, lightly beaten

¾ bunch fresh parsley, chopped

1½ teaspoons Ragin Cajun spice mix†

*If necessary, add more crumbled bread a tablespoon at a time to make a firm loaf.
†Ragin Cajun is the brand name of a spice blend Louis recommends. If you can't find this particular brand, substitute 1 teaspoon cayenne pepper.

1. Preheat the oven to 350 degrees. Lightly oil a 9 × 13-inch roasting pan.

2. Coat the pork tenderloin with 1½ teaspoons black pepper. Sauté the pork tenderloin in 2 tablespoons of corn oil until it is brown on all sides. Take it out of the pan and place it in a roasting pan. Bake for 6 to 10 minutes. Remove the tenderloin from the oven and turn the oven up to 375 degrees.

3. In the same pan, add the last tablespoon of corn oil and sauté the onion for 5 minutes. Add the red pepper and sauté for 5 minutes. Add the mushrooms and sauté for 5 minutes. Add the wine, cooking the mixture until the moisture is almost evaporated. Add the rosemary, thyme, marjoram, and allspice. Simmer for 5 minutes. Take off the heat and set aside.

4. In a large bowl, combine the ground pork and ground veal with the prosciutto, bread, garlic powder, barbecue sauce, eggs, parsley, spice mix, and sautéed vegetables. Mix well.

5. In the roasting pan, form half the meat mixture into a loaf with a depression in the middle large enough to hold the tenderloin. Place the tenderloin in the middle of the mixture and cover it with the remaining meat. Sprinkle the remaining ½ teaspoon black pepper on the top.

6. Bake 1 hour. Let the loaf sit for 10 minutes before serving. Make sure you use a very sharp knife to cut through the pork tenderloin when slicing.

Safari-Garden Meatloaf

·

Douglas Popwell II
LACEY, WASHINGTON

"I enjoy cooking and being creative. I usually put everything but the kitchen sink in most of my dishes."
 —Douglas Popwell II

WMHQ Note: We're different. We put all our dishes in the kitchen sink. This is an unusual loaf. The vegetables in the filling are put into the loaf frozen, then cook perfectly along with the meatloaf.

Serves 6 to 8

Meatloaf

1 pound bacon strips
1½ pounds lean ground beef
½ large red bell pepper, finely chopped
½ medium onion, finely chopped
2 slices multi-grain wheat bread, torn into small pieces*
1 large egg, lightly beaten
3 large garlic cloves, finely chopped
1 tablespoon Tiger sauce†

2 tablespoons dark molasses
1 tablespoon Worcestershire sauce
2 tablespoons ketchup
1 teaspoon dry mustard
½ teaspoon dried basil
½ teaspoon dried savory
¼ teaspoon dried rosemary
¼ teaspoon black pepper

*If necessary, add more bread pieces a tablespoon at a time to make a firm loaf.
†Tiger sauce can be found in the liquid spice section of most supermarkets. It's usually near the steak sauces.

Filling

1½ cups fresh (or frozen)
   broccoli florets
1 cup frozen corn

1 cup frozen peas
1½ cups grated cheddar cheese

1. Preheat the oven to 350 degrees. Lightly oil a 9 × 5 × 3-inch loaf pan.

2. Place the bacon strips on a cookie sheet with sides and bake until golden brown and limp, about 8 to 10 minutes. Drain and let cool. Chop the bacon into small pieces and set aside.

3. In a large bowl, combine the ground beef, red pepper, onion, bread, egg, garlic, Tiger sauce, molasses, Worcestershire sauce, ketchup, mustard, and herbs and spices. Add the bacon. Mix well.

4. Take two-thirds of the meat mixture and line the bottom and sides of the prepared pan so that it forms a pocket shape.

5. Add the broccoli, corn, peas, and cheese. Top with the remaining one-third meat mixture to enclose the loaf.

6. Bake for 1 hour or until done. Drain the excess drippings and let it sit for 15 minutes. Transfer the loaf to a platter and serve.

Meatloaf Florentine

JEWELL P. BUECHLER

FOUNTAIN HILLS, ARIZONA

WMHQ Note: This is an elegant loaf! Ricotta cheese, nutmeg, and Sauterne wine make this an unusual blend of flavors. And of course, any loaf with sausage has to taste good.

SERVES 8 to 10

Filling

3 tablespoons butter, melted
1 cup ricotta cheese
1 10-ounce package frozen
  chopped spinach, thawed,
  squeezed dry, and chopped

½ teaspoon grated nutmeg
¼ cup grated Parmesan cheese

Meatloaf

1 pound bulk pork sausage
1 4-ounce can mushrooms,
  stems and pieces with juice
1 4-ounce package Knorr
  vegetable soup mix

1½ pounds ground beef
2 cups plain bread crumbs*
2 large eggs, lightly beaten
⅔ cup Sauterne wine

*If necessary, add more bread crumbs a tablespoon at a time to make a firm loaf.

Mushroom Green Sauce

4 large fresh spinach leaves,
  finely chopped
¼ cup Sauterne wine

1 10¾-ounce can cream of
  mushroom soup

Garnish

½ teaspoon paprika

1. Preheat the oven to 350 degrees. Thoroughly oil a 10-inch Bundt pan.

2. In a bowl, combine the butter, ricotta cheese, spinach, nutmeg, and Parmesan cheese. Blend until smooth and creamy. Set aside.

3. In a food processor or blender, finely grind the pork sausage. Add the mushrooms with juice and the vegetable soup mix to the ground sausage and process for 15 seconds.

4. In a large bowl, combine the ground beef and the sausage mixture. Stir in the bread crumbs, eggs, and wine. Mix well.

5. Press half the meatloaf mixture into the prepared pan.

6. Spread the filling over the top of the mixture, pressing well into the fluted sides. Top with the remaining meatloaf mixture.

7. Bake for 1 hour or until done. Drain off any excess liquid.

8. Meanwhile, in a blender mix the sauce ingredients until smooth. Pour into a medium saucepan and heat over medium-low heat 10 minutes before the meatloaf is ready to serve.

9. Let the meatloaf sit for 10 minutes. Turn the loaf out onto a large serving platter. Spoon some of the sauce over the top of the meatloaf. Sprinkle with paprika for garnish. Serve extra sauce with meatloaf.

Company Meatloaf with Onion Mushroom Sauce

Richard Correlle

AMESBURY, MASSACHUSETTS

WMHQ Note: Richard Correlle wowed the judges at the 1991 Northeast Regional Cookoff with this recipe. A salesman from Massachusetts, he loves to experiment with his recipes. This prizewinner was the result of months of experimentation. He and his wife hosted a murder mystery at their home one evening, and this meatloaf was served for the first time. I hope the meatloaf wasn't a suspect.

Meatloaf

2½ pounds ground sirloin or lean ground beef

1 pound sweet Italian sausage, casing removed

2 large Spanish onions

2 leeks (white part only), rinsed and chopped

2 celery stalks

6 large garlic cloves

2 medium carrots

1 cup heavy cream

1 cup plain bread crumbs*

4 extra-large eggs, lightly beaten

*If necessary, add more bread crumbs a tablespoon at a time to make a firm loaf.

2 teaspoons coarsely ground
 black pepper
1 teaspoon dry mustard
1 teaspoon dried basil
1 teaspoon finely minced fresh
 rosemary, or ½ teaspoon
 dried

1 teaspoon salt
1 tablespoon dried oregano
1 tablespoon Jamaican
 Pickapeppa sauce (optional)
4 ounces salt pork, rind
 removed, cut into 3 slices
1 pound beef back ribs

Onion Mushroom Sauce

1 extra-large Spanish onion,
 thickly sliced
3 tablespoons butter
½ pound large mushrooms,
 thickly sliced
1 cup dry white wine
1 6-ounce can condensed beef
 consommé

1 tablespoon tomato paste
1 ¾-ounce package brown
 gravy mix
½ cup cold water
2 tablespoons heavy cream
1 tablespoon port wine
⅛ teaspoon black pepper
¼ cup chopped fresh parsley

1. Preheat the oven to 350 degrees. Lightly oil a 10 × 13-inch roasting pan.

2. Process the ground sirloin in a food processor for 15 seconds. Place the sirloin in a bowl and set aside. Process the sausage for 15 seconds and add to the sirloin.

3. In the food processor, finely chop the onions, leeks, celery, garlic, and carrots. Add half the processed vegetables to the meat mixture.

4. In a small bowl, combine the cream and bread crumbs; stir and set aside.

5. Add the eggs, herbs and spices, hot sauce, and bread crumb mixture to the meat and vegetables. Mix well.

(continued)

6. Form the meat mixture into a loaf and place it in the prepared pan, leaving at least 1½ inches on all sides. Place the salt pork on top of the meatloaf and surround it with the beef ribs.

7. Place the loaf in the oven, uncovered. After 30 minutes, spoon the remaining vegetables around the meatloaf and ribs. Bake another 1½ hours or until done. When the loaf is done, discard the bones. Using 2 spatulas, remove the meatloaf from the pan. Let it sit 15 minutes before slicing.

8. While the meat is cooking, prepare the sauce. In a medium saucepan, sauté the onion in the butter for 3 to 4 minutes over medium heat. Add the mushrooms and sauté for another 8 to 10 minutes. Set aside.

9. Place the roasting pan with the drippings on the stove. Add the wine and simmer over medium-high heat for 10 to 12 minutes, stirring well.

10. Using a fine strainer, strain the drippings into a small bowl, pressing the vegetables with the back of a spoon to squeeze out the juice. Let the drippings stand for 5 minutes. Skim off the grease and pour the remaining juice into the pan with the mushrooms. Stir in the consommé concentrate and tomato paste, turning the heat to medium-high.

11. In a jar, stir the brown gravy mix with the cold water. Shake well. Add the gravy to the saucepan, stirring well. When the sauce begins to bubble, reduce the heat and simmer for 2 to 3 minutes.

12. Add the cream and port. Simmer another 2 minutes, adding the black pepper.

13. Slice the meatloaf, pouring a few spoonfuls of sauce over each slice. Pour the rest of the sauce into a gravy boat. Garnish the meatloaf with the parsley and serve.

Chapter 7

Poultry Loaves

*W*hen we started the Great American Meatloaf Contest in 1991, we had only one category: Meatloaves. After receiving letters (and recipes) from people who wanted a poultry category, we figured, Why not? How many people actually make poultry loaves? A lot more than we thought!

With the trend toward healthier eating, poultry loaf entries came in from all around the country. Here are some pointers for making poultry loaves:

1. To keep your loaf moist, add sour cream or mayonnaise to the mixture. If you're concerned about adding extra fat and calories, use reduced-fat products. Many of the entrants in this category used applesauce as a flavor enhancer. It's also a terrific way to keep the loaves moist. It's an idea we've adapted in some of our meatloaves as well.

2. Several recipes call for egg substitute. They do the job—you can't tell the difference in these loaves. And egg substitute is lower in cholesterol.

3. Keep an eye on your loaf. Since ovens vary in temperature, it is especially important to remove poultry loaves from the oven as soon as they are done. All meat continues to cook when removed from the oven. So take the poultry loaves out a few minutes early so you don't overcook them.

4. For poultry loaf leftovers, wrap them as soon as possible in air-tight containers or plastic wrap to ensure they stay moist.

Even if you've never thought of making a poultry loaf, give some of these a try. They're inexpensive, healthy, and delicious.

Genevieve's Turkey Loaf

•

GENEVIEVE KUKICH

NORWICH, CONNECTICUT

WMHQ Note: This recipe uses one of the great culinary inventions of the twentieth century: sloppy Joe mix. My fondest memories of elementary school lunches were Sloppy Joe Days.

SERVES 8 to 10

Loaf

3 pounds ground turkey
1 cup crumbled saltine
 crackers*
2 large eggs, lightly beaten, or
 equivalent in egg substitute
¼ cup finely chopped onion

1 envelope (1½ ounces)
 sloppy Joe mix (any brand)
½ teaspoon pepper
½ teaspoon salt

Topping

3 strips bacon, uncooked

1. Preheat the oven to 350 degrees. Lightly oil a 9 × 13-inch baking dish.

2. In a large bowl, combine all the ingredients and mix well.

3. Form the mixture into a loaf and place in the prepared baking dish. Place the 3 strips of bacon on top of the loaf. Cover the baking dish with aluminum foil.

4. Bake for 1 hour or until done. Let the loaf sit for 10 minutes before slicing.

*If necessary, add more cracker crumbs a tablespoon at a time to make a firm loaf.

"Smart Choice" Poultry Loaf

—————————————•—————————————

LANE NEWMAN
FORT LAUDERDALE, FLORIDA

"This is an old family recipe, which I have modified to reflect today's healthy lifestyle, with reduced sodium and fat levels."   —LANE NEWMAN

WMHQ Note: The use of reduced-sodium beef bouillon cubes is an excellent idea for adding flavor without increasing the amount of salt.

SERVES 6 to 8

2 reduced-sodium beef
   bouillon cubes
½ cup boiling water
1 large egg, lightly beaten
¼ teaspoon black pepper
½ teaspoon dried basil
½ teaspoon dried thyme
¼ cup ketchup (reduced-
   sodium preferred)

2 teaspoons Dijon mustard
1½ cups fresh whole wheat
   bread crumbs*
½ cup chopped celery
½ cup chopped onion
4 ounce package sharp cheddar
   cheese (reduced-fat
   preferred), shredded
2 pounds ground turkey

*If necessary, add more bread crumbs a tablespoon at a time to make a firm loaf.

1. Preheat the oven to 350 degrees. Lightly oil a 10 × 13-inch roasting pan.

2. Dissolve the bouillon cubes in boiling water.

3. In a large bowl, combine the egg, pepper, basil, thyme, ketchup, mustard, and bread crumbs. Mix well.

4. Add the bouillon to the ingredients in the bowl.

5. Mix in the celery, onion, and cheese. Add the ground turkey and mix well.

6. Form into 2 loaves and place in the prepared roasting pan. (Note: We made this as one loaf and it worked fine. It's your choice.)

7. Bake uncovered for 1 hour and 15 minutes, or until done. Let the loaf sit covered with aluminum foil for 10 minutes before slicing.

Turkey and Eggplant Loaf

———————————•———————————

KIM BOUCHER

WATERBURY, CONNECTICUT

WMHQ Note: In all the vegetable kingdom there is nothing as attractive as eggplant. That deep purple color really looks great . . . until you cut it open. Then it looks like a vegetable. This is a delicious turkey loaf and the eggplant helps keep it moist during cooking.

SERVES 6

1 small eggplant
½ cup V-8 juice
¼ teaspoon dried thyme
¼ teaspoon dried sage
¼ teaspoon dried rosemary

1 pound ground turkey
1 medium onion, chopped
1 garlic clove, minced
½ cup cracked wheat*

1. Preheat the oven to 350 degrees. Lightly oil a 9 × 5 × 3-inch loaf pan.

2. Peel the eggplant and remove the seeds. Cut the eggplant into 1-inch cubes. In a large saucepan of boiling water, place the eggplant cubes and boil for 3 minutes. Drain and mash.

3. In a large bowl, combine all the remaining ingredients, add the mashed eggplant, and mix well.

4. Press the poultry mixture into the prepared pan.

5. Bake for 45 minutes or until done. Let the loaf sit for 10 minutes before slicing.

*If necessary, add more cracked wheat a tablespoon at a time to make a firm loaf.

Chili-Chicken Loaf

———•———

KATE MESSER

DANBURY, CONNECTICUT

WMHQ Note: This recipe has just the right balance of tortilla chips and kidney beans. When we made this a second time, we bumped up the amount of chili powder.

SERVES 4 to 6

1 pound ground chicken
1 small onion, chopped
1 garlic clove, minced
1 cup finely crushed tortilla
  chips*
½ cup V-8 juice
1 16-ounce can whole kernel
  corn, drained
1 15 ½-ounce can red kidney
  beans, drained and rinsed

1 tablespoon chili powder, or
  more if desired
¼ teaspoon black pepper
¼ teaspoon cayenne pepper
1 tablespoon chopped fresh
  parsley
1 tablespoon chopped fresh
  basil
1 cup shredded cheddar cheese

1. Preheat the oven to 350 degrees. Lightly coat a 9 × 5 × 3-inch loaf pan with nonstick cooking spray.

2. In a large bowl, combine all the ingredients except the cheese and mix well.

3. Press the poultry mixture into the loaf pan.

4. Top with the cheese.

5. Bake for 35 to 40 minutes, or until done. Let the loaf sit for 10 minutes before slicing.

*If necesary, add more chip crumbs a tablespoon at a time to make a firm loaf.

Spa Poultry Loaf

———•———

Barbara J. Rau

BURLINGTON, CONNECTICUT

WMHQ Note: This loaf has a good texture and the carrots and lemon give it a refreshing taste. To zest a lemon, you can purchase a lemon zester or use a sharp knife to remove only the top colored layer of the lemon. Make sure you don't use the bitter white part right below the skin.

SERVES 6 to 8

2 slices bread, toasted, then processed in a food processor or blender into crumbs*
½ cup wheat germ
½ cup club soda
¼ cup egg substitute
1¼ cups shredded carrots
1 medium onion, chopped

1 tablespoon Worcestershire sauce
¼ teaspoon black pepper
¼ teaspoon celery salt
¼ teaspoon dried oregano
1 teaspoon Dijon mustard
Zest of 1 lemon
Juice of ½ lemon
2 pounds ground turkey

1. Preheat the oven to 350 degrees. Lightly coat a 9 × 5 × 3-inch pan with nonstick cooking spray.

2. In a large bowl, mix all the ingredients, adding the ground turkey last.

3. Place the poultry mixture in the loaf pan.

4. Bake for 1½ hours or until done. Let the loaf sit for 10 minutes before slicing.

*Or use stale white bread. If necessary, add more bread crumbs a tablespoon at a time to make a firm loaf.

Holiday Memories Turkey Loaf

— • —

PAM JONES
SHAKER HEIGHTS, OHIO

"Last summer while driving to Cape Cod, I was thinking about your contest and tried to come up with something new and different. As my husband and I drove past a cranberry bog, I remembered a beef meatloaf roll I made years ago that was filled with a blue cheese and mushroom filling. I thought, 'Why not try a turkey loaf rolled with a filling of cranberry sauce and stuffing?' The idea for my Holiday Memories Turkey Loaf was born and the result was delicious! It has become one of my family's most requested entrees." —PAM JONES

SERVES 6

Filling

½ cup chopped celery
½ cup chopped onion
1 tablespoon butter
½ cup sliced fresh mushrooms

¼ cup water
¼ cup chopped fresh parsley
1 cup Pepperidge Farm
   stuffing mix

Loaf

1⅓ pounds ground turkey
1 cup fresh bread crumbs*
¼ cup chopped onion

½ teaspoon garlic salt
¼ cup milk
1 large egg, lightly beaten

(*continued*)

*If necessary, add more bread crumbs a tablespoon at a time to make a firm loaf.

Sauce

⅓ cup crushed cranberry sauce
  (*not* whole berry sauce)

1. Preheat the oven to 350 degrees. Lightly oil a 9 × 13-inch baking dish.

2. In a large skillet sauté the celery and onion in the butter until tender, about 4 to 6 minutes. Add the mushrooms and sauté another 3 to 4 minutes. The mixture should be spreadable, not dry.

3. Add the water and bring to a boil; stir in the parsley and stuffing mix. Cover and remove from the heat. (If the mushrooms do not release much moisture, you may need to add 1 to 2 tablespoons of hot water.)

4. In a large bowl, combine the loaf ingredients.

5. Spray a 10 × 16-inch piece of aluminum foil with nonstick cooking spray. Spread the poultry mixture on top of the foil to form a 12 × 8-inch rectangle. Spread the cranberry sauce on top of the poultry loaf mixture. Then spread the stuffing mixture on top of the cranberry sauce.

6. Roll up the loaf jellyroll style, starting with the long side (for a long loaf). Wrap the foil tightly around the roll and place in the prepared baking dish. (See page 94 for roll-up instructions.)

7. Bake for 45 minutes. Open the foil and continue baking for 15 minutes or until done. Let the loaf sit for 10 minutes. Unwrap the foil and serve.

Lo-Fat Tasty Turkey Loaf

•

Carol Dykstra

BRAINTREE, MASSACHUSETTS

WMHQ Note: When we tried this loaf a second time, we increased the amount of pickle relish and horseradish-mustard. As with all of the recipes in this chapter, seasoning is everything. This one has plenty of good flavors. Delicious hot or cold.

S E R V E S 4

Loaf

1¼ pounds ground turkey
1 large egg, lightly beaten
½ cup plain low-salt bread
   crumbs*
1 teaspoon onion powder
½ cup sweet pickle relish
1 teaspoon dried sage

2 tablespoons prepared
   horseradish-mustard, or 1
   tablespoon prepared
   horseradish mixed with 1
   tablespoon Dijon mustard
½ teaspoon ground ginger

Topping

¼ cup barbecue sauce

(continued)

*If necessary, add more bread crumbs a tablespoon at a time to make a firm loaf.

1. Preheat the oven to 350 degrees. Grease a 9 × 5 × 3-inch loaf with 1 teaspoon olive oil.

2. In a large bowl, mix all the loaf ingredients.

3. Place the poultry mixture in the prepared pan.

4. Spread the top of the meatloaf with barbecue sauce.

5. Bake for 40 minutes or until done. Let the loaf sit for 10 minutes before slicing.

Tangy Turkey Loaf
•

Ann M. Bake

NEW PORT RICHEY, FLORIDA

WMHQ Note: Tangy is a word like zesty. *I've vowed never to use it in a sentence. But this loaf really is the ''T'' word.*

SERVES 3 to 4

Topping

¼ teaspoon Worcestershire
  sauce
1 tablespoon ketchup

1 teaspoon prepared mustard
1 tablespoon light brown
  sugar, packed

Loaf

1 small Vidalia or other sweet
  onion
¼ large red bell pepper
1 tablespoon chopped fresh
  parsley
1¼ pounds ground turkey
1 tablespoon Worcestershire
  sauce
½ teaspoon salt
1 teaspoon garlic salt

1 teaspoon seasoned salt
⅛ teaspoon black pepper
1 tablespoon light brown
  sugar, packed
1 tablespoon grated Romano
  cheese
2 cups plain bread crumbs*
¼ cup tomato juice
1 large egg, lightly beaten

1. Preheat the oven to 325 degrees. Lightly oil an 8 × 10-inch baking dish.

2. In a small bowl, mix the topping ingredients and set aside.

3. In a food processor, chop the onion, red pepper, and parsley, or dice by hand. Place the chopped vegetables in a large bowl. Add the turkey, Worcestershire sauce, salt, garlic salt, seasoned salt, and black pepper. Mix thoroughly.

4. Add the brown sugar, Romano cheese, bread crumbs, tomato juice, and egg. Mix well.

5. Form the turkey mixture into a loaf. Place in the prepared baking dish. Poke several holes in the top of the loaf with your finger, then pour the topping over the poultry loaf.

6. Bake 1¼ hours. Let the loaf sit for 10 minutes before serving.

*If necessary, add more bread crumbs a tablespoon at a time to make a firm loaf.

Savory Poultry Loaf

———————•———————

AMELIA E. WILCZAK

SYRACUSE, NEW YORK

"For a more decorative presentation of the loaf, double the recipe. Then, spray a 6-cup ring mold with nonstick cooking spray. Press the loaf into the mold and bake according to directions. Unmold and garnish the center with your favorite stuffing or steamed vegetables."
                                                            —AMELIA E. WILCZAK

WMHQ Note: This is a presentation idea you can use with most of the other poultry loaves.

SERVES 6

1¼ pounds ground turkey
¾ cup plain bread crumbs*
¾ cup low-fat or skim milk
½ cup chopped onion
1 teaspoon dry mustard
½ cup chopped green bell
   pepper
1 tablespoon white wine
   Worcestershire sauce
1 teaspoon poultry seasoning

¼ teaspoon minced garlic
1 4-ounce can mushroom
   pieces, drained
2 large eggs, lightly beaten, or
   ½ cup egg substitute
½ cup grated carrot
⅛ teaspoon salt
⅛ teaspoon black pepper

*If necessary, add more bread crumbs a tablespoon at a time to make a firm loaf.

1. Preheat the oven to 350 degrees. Lightly coat a 9 × 5 × 3-inch loaf pan with nonstick cooking spray.

2. In a large bowl, mix all the ingredients thoroughly.

3. Press the mixture in the prepared pan.

4. Bake 1¼ hours. Let the loaf sit for 10 minutes before slicing.

Skinnied Down Turkey Loaf

•

NANCY C. ROSE

FRAMINGHAM, MASSACHUSETTS

"I have recently lost 35 pounds, but not my appetite for delicious tasting food. This original poultry loaf recipe allows me to enjoy a healthy, tasty, quick-to-prepare and inexpensive dinner. What more could I ask? Maybe to lose another pound!"
—NANCY ROSE

WMHQ Note: This recipe has no real binding, but it holds together beautifully. If you like dill pickle, increase the amount by 1 or 2 tablespoons.

(*continued*)

SERVES 6 to 8

3 pounds ground turkey
3 tablespoons chopped onion
3 tablespoons chopped celery
3 tablespoons chopped fresh
  parsley
3 tablespoons chopped dill
  pickle
3 tablespoons Worcestershire
  sauce

1½ teaspoons salt
¾ teaspoon dry mustard
¾ teaspoon black pepper
¾ teaspoon ground sage
¾ teaspoon dried dill
¾ teaspoon garlic salt

1. Preheat the oven to 350 degrees. Lightly oil a 9 × 5 × 3-inch loaf pan.

2. In a large bowl, combine all the ingredients and mix well.

3. Place the mixture in the prepared pan.

4. Bake for 1 hour or until done. Let the loaf sit 10 minutes before slicing.

Good 'n Spicy Poultry Loaf

FREDDA HUTCHISON

SAN FRANCISCO, CALIFORNIA

"This was my mother's recipe, and I have modified it to be lower in salt, fat, and cholesterol while keeping it flavorful and spicy. The leftovers make great sandwiches."
—FREDDA HUTCHISON

SERVES 6

Loaf

2 pounds ground turkey
2 large eggs, lightly beaten
2 slices whole wheat bread,*
  crumbled
½ 14-ounce jar salsa
1 large onion, diced
2 celery stalks, diced

1 14-ounce can low-salt kernel
  corn, drained
1 large carrot, grated
½ teaspoon salt
2 packages Herb-Ox low-
  sodium beef flavoring
⅛ teaspoon dried thyme

Topping

½ 14-ounce jar salsa

1. Preheat the oven to 350 degrees. Lightly oil a 9 × 5 × 3-inch loaf pan.
2. In a large bowl, mix all of the ingredients.
3. Form the mixture into a loaf and place it in the prepared pan.
4. Refrigerate the loaf for at least 1 hour before baking.
5. Pour the topping over the loaf and bake for 1½ hours or until done.
6. Let the loaf sit for 10 minutes before serving.

*If necessary, add more bread crumbs a tablespoon at a time to make a firm loaf.

1992 THIRD PLACE—THE GREAT AMERICAN MEATLOAF NATIONAL RECIPE CONTEST, POULTRY CATEGORY

African Bobotie with Poultry

PATRICIA WOODWARD

SOUTH SAN FRANCISCO, CALIFORNIA

WMHQ Note: This is an exotic loaf. The curry powder, vinegar, raisins, and almonds make this taste unlike any other loaf we've tried. And we tried over 600 of them. Have you ever tried 600 meatloaves in three months? Many of them twice? When one stands out as much as this one does, it must mean it's delicious.

SERVES 6

3 slices day-old bread*
1½ cups milk
1½ pounds ground chicken
2 medium onions, chopped
1 garlic clove, minced
½ cup almonds
½ cup raisins

1 tablespoon sugar
1 teaspoon salt
1 teaspoon curry powder
⅛ teaspoon black pepper
1 tablespoon vinegar
1 teaspoon lemon juice
2 large eggs, lightly beaten

*If necessary, add more bread a little at a time to make a firm loaf.

1. Preheat the oven to 350 degrees. Lightly oil an 11 × 7-inch baking dish.

2. Soak the bread in the milk. Squeeze the milk from the bread, and reserve the milk.

3. In a large bowl, combine all the remaining ingredients except 1 egg.

4. Press the mixture into the prepared baking dish.

5. Add enough milk to the reserved milk to make ¾ cup. Beat together the milk and the remaining egg.

6. Pour the milk and egg mixture over the poultry loaf. Bake for 1 hour or until done. Let the loaf sit for 10 minutes before slicing.

"To Die(t) For" Turkey Loaf

GAYLE NYREN

LOS ANGELES, CALIFORNIA

WMHQ Note: This poultry loaf has an excellent texture. The cranberries not only add color but also help keep it moist. We received a lot of recipes in 1992 that included cranberries. This was one of the best.

SERVES 6 to 8

Loaf

1 large egg or egg white
½ cup low-salt chicken broth
1 teaspoon garlic powder
1–2 teaspoons poultry
    seasoning
½ teaspoon black pepper
1 cup packaged stuffing mix or
    1 cup rolled oats*

1 large carrot, diced
1 celery stalk, diced
½ medium onion, diced
6 fresh mushrooms, diced
1½ pounds ground turkey
⅓ cup crushed cranberry sauce

Topping

¼ cup crushed cranberry sauce

*If necessary, add more stuffing mix or oats a tablespoon at a time to make a firm loaf.

1. Preheat the oven to 350 degrees. Lightly oil a 9 × 5 × 3-inch loaf pan.

2. Beat together the egg or egg white, broth, garlic powder, poultry seasoning, and black pepper.

3. Add the stuffing mix or rolled oats and let soak for 3 minutes.

4. Add the carrot, celery, onion, and mushrooms.

5. Add the turkey and cranberry sauce.

6. Press into the prepared loaf pan. Spread with cranberry sauce for topping. Bake for 1½ hours or until done. Let the loaf sit for 10 minutes.

Stuffed Poultry Loaf Italiano

●

SUSAN MCDOWELL

DALLAS, TEXAS

WMHQ Note: This is a really tasty poultry loaf, whose flavors rely on a good use of Italian spices and seasonings. As with most loaves that have a lot of seasoning, it's a good idea to refrigerate the mixture for an hour before baking—it gives the ingredients the time to blend.

SERVES 6 to 8

Loaf

1¼ cups milk
2 large eggs, lightly beaten
1¼ cups plain bread crumbs*
2 teaspoons dried oregano
2 teaspoons cayenne pepper

2 garlic cloves, chopped
¼ cup grated Parmesan cheese
1 teaspoon salt
2 pounds ground chicken or
    turkey

Filling

6 ounces mozzarella cheese,
    shredded

1 2-ounce can mushrooms,
    drained and chopped

Topping

¼ cup prepared spaghetti
    sauce

2 ounces mozzarella cheese,
    shredded

*If necessary, add more bread crumbs a tablespoon at a time to make a firm loaf.

1. Preheat the oven to 350 degrees. Lightly oil a 9 × 5 × 3-inch loaf pan.

2. In a large bowl, combine the milk, eggs, bread crumbs, oregano, cayenne, garlic, Parmesan cheese, and salt.

3. Add the meat and combine thoroughly. Divide the poultry mixture in half. Form a 9-inch loaf with the first half, making a depression in the top of the loaf.

4. In another bowl, mix the filling ingredients. Place the filling in the loaf's depression.

5. Place the reserved poultry mixture on top of the filling. Put the loaf in the prepared pan.

6. Bake for 1 hour. Take out of the oven and top with the spaghetti sauce and mozzarella cheese.

7. Return the loaf to the oven and bake 15 minutes longer. Let the loaf sit for 10 minutes before slicing.

**1992 SECOND PLACE—THE GREAT AMERICAN MEATLOAF
NATIONAL RECIPE CONTEST, POULTRY CATEGORY**

Jake's Meatloaf

NANCY ANN KASTNER
TALLAHASSEE, FLORIDA

*WMHQ Note: All of the judges loved the taste of this loaf. Placing a raw
egg in the middle of the loaf is an interesting idea that helps keep the poultry
loaf moist. We tried it without the egg and it was still great. It's your choice.*

SERVES 6 to 8

1 pound ground turkey
1 pound turkey sausage*
1 cup finely crushed unsalted
  crackers†
1 small onion, finely chopped
1 tablespoon finely chopped
  jalapeño pepper
1 teaspoon Spice Islands salt-
  free lemon-herb seasoning
1 teaspoon garlic salt

1 teaspoon Italian seasoning
½ teaspoon black pepper
3 tablespoons Worcestershire
  sauce
2 large eggs, lightly beaten
1 cup milk
½ cup water

---

*There are a variety of turkey sausages available. They are spicy and a great addition to
poultry loaves. They can usually be found at the deli counter of your local supermarket.
†If necessary, add more cracker crumbs a tablespoon at a time to make a firm loaf.

1. Preheat the oven to 350 degrees. Lightly coat a 9-inch square pan with olive oil.

2. In a large bowl, combine the turkey and turkey sausage until well blended. Add the crackers, onion, pepper, and spices. Then add 2 tablespoons of Worcestershire sauce, 1 egg, and the milk. Mix well.

3. Form the mixture into an oval loaf and place into the prepared pan.

4. Hollow out an oval pocket deep in the center of the loaf. Crack 1 egg and carefully drop it into the hole. Close the opening by gently shaping the loaf over it.

5. Sprinkle the remaining tablespoon of Worcestershire sauce over the loaf, and pour the water into the pan around the loaf.

6. Bake for 1 hour or until done. Let the loaf sit for 10 minutes before slicing.

Wilson's Baked Chicken Loaf

---•---

KENNETH WILSON
BRIDGEPORT, CONNECTICUT

WMHQ Note: Chicken broth and garlic are ancient remedies for what ails you. So the next time you're feeling poorly, skip the chicken soup and have a slice of this poultry loaf.

SERVES 8

1 6-ounce package Pepperidge Farm Wild Rice and Mushroom Stuffing Mix*
1 13¾-ounce can chicken broth
3 pounds ground chicken
1 small onion, chopped
1 garlic clove, chopped
½ teaspoon black pepper
½ teaspoon salt
1 tablespoon curry powder
½ cup egg substitute
½ cup hot water

1. Preheat the oven to 350 degrees. Lightly coat a 14½ × 10½ × 2-inch baking pan with nonstick cooking spray.

---

*If necessary, add more stuffing a tablespoon at a time to make a firm loaf.

2. In a bowl, combine the stuffing mix and chicken broth. Blend well and set aside.

3. In a large bowl, combine the chicken, onion, garlic, pepper, salt, and curry powder. Blend well and then mix in the egg substitute. Add the stuffing and broth mixture and blend all the ingredients thoroughly.

4. Form the poultry mixture into a 12 × 5½-inch loaf. Place the loaf in the prepared pan.

5. Bake 1 hour and then add the hot water. Pour the water around the chicken, not on top of it. Bake another 30 minutes or until done.

6. Let the loaf sit for 10 minutes before slicing.

1992 FIRST PLACE—THE GREAT AMERICAN MEATLOAF NATIONAL RECIPE CONTEST, POULTRY CATEGORY

Chicken Cordon Bleu with Mushroom Sauce

PAMELA SEAMAN
WILLIMANTIC, CONNECTICUT

"My greatest pleasure from cooking is watching my twelve-year-old son eat. He's already asked me if, when he's old enough, I could teach his wife how to cook. The day I made up this loaf, I was supposed to be making an appetizer using chopped chicken breasts. Instead, I bought ground chicken. When my son asked me what I was making for dinner, I just said, "Chicken." He asked if I could make the kind stuffed with ham and cheese. I explained that I didn't have chicken breasts, just the kind to make a meatloaf. He suggested that I stuff a meatloaf with the ham and cheese. I made two different loaves, and this one won my family's approval."

—PAMELA SEAMAN

SERVES 6 to 8

Loaf

1½ pounds ground chicken
2 large eggs, lightly beaten
1 cup fresh bread crumbs*
2 tablespoons milk or half-
   and-half

1 tablespoon chopped fresh
   parsley
1 teaspoon salt
½ teaspoon black pepper
½ teaspoon ground allspice

Filling

4 slices low-fat Swiss cheese

4 slices low-fat turkey ham

Mushroom Sauce

4 tablespoons butter or
   margarine
1 cup sliced mushrooms
1 tablespoon minced shallots
1 chicken bouillon cube

½ cup dry white wine
1 tablespoon cornstarch
1 cup heavy cream or half-
   and-half

1. Preheat the oven to 375 degrees. Lightly coat a 9 × 5 × 3-inch loaf pan with nonstick cooking spray.

2. In a large bowl, mix all the loaf ingredients.

3. Put the mixture on a lightly oiled piece of aluminum foil resting on a cookie sheet, and press the mixture into a 7 × 10-inch rectangle. Place the ham and cheese on the rectangle. Cover with another piece of aluminum foil and refrigerate for 1 hour until firm.

4. Roll up the loaf, starting at the smaller side using the foil to lift. Seal the edges and ends of the loaf. (See page 94 for roll-up instructions.)

(*continued*)

---

*If necessary, add more bread crumbs a tablespoon at a time to make a firm loaf.

5. Place in the prepared pan. Bake for 1 hour, or until the top is brown and sides pull away.

6. In a medium skillet, melt the butter over medium heat. Cook the mushrooms and shallots until soft, about 3 minutes. Add the bouillon cube and wine.

7. In a small bowl mix the cornstarch and cream or half-and-half until smooth. Add to the mushroom mixture and cook until thickened.

8. Let the loaf sit for 10 minutes before slicing. Serve with the sauce.

Casa de Chotchkes Meatloaf

STELLA NEVES

GLASTONBURY, CONNECTICUT

WMHQ Note: The Neves family have a cabin in the Berkshires named Casa de Chotchkes (aka: House with Lots of Stuff). Stella describes chotchkes as things left over from other homes they've had over the years and they couldn't bring themselves to throw out. The Neves have four children and this is one of Stella's most requested dishes.

We used more pesto sauce (4 tablespoons) than the recipe listed.

SERVES 4

Loaf

1¼ pounds ground turkey
1 large onion, chopped
1 cup seasoned bread crumbs*
2 large eggs, lightly beaten
¼ cup canned tomato sauce

2 tablespoons prepared Pesto
sauce (see page 181 or use
commercial Pesto)
1 cup shredded mozzarella
cheese

Topping

¼ cup canned tomato sauce

1. Preheat the oven to 350 degrees. Lightly oil a nonstick cookie sheet with sides.

2. In a large bowl, combine the turkey, onion, bread crumbs, eggs, and tomato sauce. Mix well.

3. On a large piece of aluminum foil, spread the mixture in a rectangular shape approximately 12 × 10 × ½ inches.

4. Spread the pesto sauce over the meat mixture.

5. Top with the shredded cheese. Leave a 1-inch margin around the loaf. This will prevent the cheese from seeping out during baking.

6. Roll up the meat mixture jellyroll style. Smooth seams with wet hands. (See page 94 for roll-up instructions.)

7. Place the loaf on the prepared cookie sheet and bake 50 minutes.

8. Pour tomato sauce over the loaf. Bake another 15 minutes. Let the loaf sit 10 minutes before slicing.

*If necessary, add more bread crumbs a tablespoon at a time to make a firm loaf.

Marjorie's Chicken Loaf

———•———

MARJORIE OHRNSTEIN

SCOTTSDALE, ARIZONA

WMHQ Note: A funny thing happened on the way to this recipe. When we made it the second time, I increased the amount of cayenne pepper. I went to answer the phone and T. K. also added more cayenne. She left to go to a meeting and another WMHQ staff member added even more cayenne. After the firemen left, we made a rule: Whoever starts the recipe finishes the recipe. If you like a spicier loaf, increase the seasonings as you desire.

SERVES 6

½ teaspoon ground cumin
½ teaspoon grated nutmeg
⅛ teaspoon ground cinnamon
⅛ teaspoon white pepper
1 teaspoon cayenne pepper
⅛ teaspoon salt
⅛ teaspoon black pepper
5 tablespoons butter
¼ cup chopped Spanish onion
¼ cup chopped green bell pepper
¼ cup chopped red bell pepper

½ cup chopped celery
½ cup chopped shallots
¼ cup chopped scallions
1½ tablespoons hot sauce
1½ tablespoons Worcestershire sauce
2 garlic cloves, minced
½ cup heavy cream
½ cup ketchup
1½ pounds ground chicken
1½ pounds ground turkey
2 large eggs, lightly beaten
1 cup plain bread crumbs*

*If necessary, add more bread crumbs a tablespoon at a time to make a firm loaf.

1. Preheat the oven to 350 degrees. Use an ungreased 9 × 13-inch baking dish.

2. In a small bowl, combine the cumin, nutmeg, cinnamon, white pepper, cayenne pepper, salt, and black pepper. Mix well and set aside.

3. In a large skillet, melt the butter and add the onion, green and red peppers, celery, shallots, scallions, hot sauce, Worcestershire sauce, and garlic. Sauté for 10 minutes.

4. Remove the skillet from the heat and add the cream and ketchup. Let this cool to room temperature.

5. In a large bowl, combine the chicken, turkey, eggs, and bread crumbs. Mix well.

6. Add the cooled vegetable mixture to the poultry mixture.

7. Place the entire mixture in the pan and form a loaf.

8. Bake for 1 hour or until done. Let the loaf sit for 10 minutes before slicing.

Chapter 8

Vegetarian Loaves

*W*hen we told people that we were including a Vegetarian Loaf category in the 1992 contest, they stared at us and said, "Vegetarian? In a meatloaf contest?"

The reason we created this category was to recognize a growing percentage of vegetarians in America. It may sound like an oxymoron to have a vegetarian meatloaf contest, but these veggie loaves adhere to our meatloaf mentality: They are easy to prepare, inexpensive, and delicious.

To you meat eaters out there, I can say only that these recipes are worth a try. If you still want to have your meatloaf and eat it too, then try these as side dishes. And to vegetarians, we hope you'll add these recipes to your list of delicious, meat-free dinners.

Here are some things we've learned about veggie loaves:

1. The basic rules of meatloaf apply. Veggie loaves require a binder such as bread crumbs, stuffing mix, or crackers. Eggs and cheese are just examples of what is used to hold the mixture together. Instead of meat, you can use grains, beans, nuts, and a wide variety of vegetables as the foundation for your recipe.

2. If you have favorite vegetable recipes, you may want to experiment in converting them to loaves. These recipes will give you ideas how that can be done.

1992 First Place—The Great American Meatloaf National Recipe Contest, Vegetarian Category

Barbecue Veggie-Burger Loaf

•

Janet H. Logan
PARADISE, CALIFORNIA

"As a new member of the Seventh-day Adventist Church, I was given many tasty vegetarian recipes to help me in my transition to a vegetarian diet. Vegetarian burger (veggie-burger) is similar in texture to ground beef. I modified a cheese loaf by adding Lipton Onion Soup mix, green pepper, chili sauce, garlic powder, and seasoned salt, and topped it off with my barbecue topping to give veggie-burger the needed zip and flavor."   —Janet Logan

WMHQ Note: Janet's recipe calls for a 20-ounce can of Worthington vegetarian burger. If this brand is not available, use any other brand of vegetarian burger and follow package directions.

Serves 6 to 8

Topping

½ cup ketchup
½ cup light brown sugar,
  packed
1 teaspoon dry mustard

¼ teaspoon ground cloves
¼ teaspoon ground allspice
¼ cup water

(continued)

Loaf

4 tablespoons margarine
1 medium onion, chopped
½ cup chopped green bell
  pepper
4 slices sourdough bread,
  cubed*
1 20-ounce can vegetarian
  burger
1 envelope (0.9 ounce) Lipton
  Onion Soup mix

1 teaspoon garlic powder
1 teaspoon seasoned salt
1 teaspoon dried sage
½ cup chili sauce
½ pound sharp cheddar
  cheese, grated
4 large eggs, lightly beaten

1. Preheat the oven to 350 degrees. Lightly coat a 2-quart casserole or two 9 × 5 × 3-inch loaf pans with nonstick vegetable spray.

2. In a small bowl, mix the topping ingredients and set aside.

3. In a large frying pan, melt the margarine and sauté the onion, green pepper, and bread cubes over medium heat until soft, about 4 to 5 minutes.

4. In a large bowl, combine the remaining loaf ingredients and add the sautéed bread cube mixture. Mix well.

5. Spread the barbecue topping over the loaf.

6. Bake uncovered for 30 to 45 minutes, or until done. Let the loaf sit for 10 minutes before slicing.

*If necessary, add more bread cubes a little at a time to make a firm loaf.

Lentil Nut Loaf

MARY RUSSELL

NEW HAVEN, CONNECTICUT

*WMHQ Note: This is a hearty, well-seasoned loaf that features lentils, an
important component of vegetarian cooking.*

SERVES 6

4 cups chicken broth
1 cup lentils
1 tablespoon finely chopped
   fresh parsley
½ cup diced onion
½ cup diced celery
¼ cup plus 2 tablespoons
   finely chopped walnuts
4 1-ounce slices whole wheat
   bread, crumbled*

2 egg whites
1 8-ounce can tomato sauce
3 tablespoons chili sauce
½ teaspoon garlic powder
½ teaspoon poultry seasoning
½ teaspoon ground sage
⅛ teaspoon salt
1 tablespoon prepared
   horseradish
⅛ teaspoon black pepper

(*continued*)

*If necessary, add more bread crumbs a tablespoon at a time to make a firm loaf.

1. Preheat the oven to 350 degrees. Lightly coat a 9 × 5 × 2-inch loaf pan with nonstick cooking spray.

2. In a medium saucepan, bring the chicken broth to a boil.

3. To the boiling broth, add the lentils and parsley and cover the saucepan. Reduce the heat to low and cook for 45 minutes. Drain the lentils and set aside to cool.

4. In a large bowl, combine the cooked lentils with the remaining ingredients. Mix well.

5. Place the mixture in the prepared pan and press down firmly with the back of a spoon.

6. Bake uncovered for 45 minutes. Let the loaf sit for 10 minutes, then invert onto a serving plate.

7. Cut into slices and serve with a mushroom, tomato, or chili sauce.

1992 Third Place—The Great American Meatloaf National Recipe Contest, Vegetarian Category

Savory Veggie Loaf

Irene Williams
ANDOVER, NEW JERSEY

WMHQ Note: This is a quick and easy loaf to prepare. The cottage cheese, cheddar cheese, and herb stuffing combine to give it a terrific consistency and flavor.

Serves 6 to 8

5 large eggs, lightly beaten, or equivalent egg substitute
1 cup shredded cheddar cheese
½ cup creamed cottage cheese
½ cup finely chopped onion
1 teaspoon dried basil
½ teaspoon salt
½ teaspoon dried sage

2 cups herb-seasoned stuffing mix*
1 cup finely chopped walnuts
1 medium red onion, finely sliced
1 8-ounce can tomato sauce
1 cup water

(continued)

*If necessary, add more stuffing mix a tablespoon at a time to make a firm loaf.

1. Preheat the oven to 350 degrees. Lightly oil a 9 × 5 × 3-inch loaf pan.

2. In a medium bowl, combine all the ingredients except the red onion, tomato sauce, and water.

3. Place the mixture in the prepared pan. Arrange the sliced onion over the loaf.

4. In a small bowl, mix the tomato sauce and water. Pour half the mixture over the veggie loaf and bake for 35 to 40 minutes. Let it sit for 10 minutes before serving.

5. Remove the loaf from the pan. Heat the remaining half of the tomato sauce mixture and serve with the veggie loaf.

Susan's Walnut Loaf

•

SUSAN KLINE
GRAND BLANC, MICHIGAN

"This recipe came from trial-and-error efforts on my part to create a vegetarian loaf for dinner that would closely resemble the meatloaf my mother used to make from beef. Since becoming a vegetarian twelve years ago, I have tried many vegetarian loaf recipes, and from this experience I devised this combination of ingredients to produce a loaf that I now use as a staple once a week."

—SUSAN KLINE

WMHQ Note: Walnuts are nature's "meat." This has a great texture and is so easy to make. Susan recommends using a food processor to chop the onion and walnuts, and to make the bread crumbs. This will make a finer textured loaf that closely resembles a loaf made from meat. It is also important to use fresh bread crumbs.

SERVES 4 to 6

Loaf

¾ cup finely chopped walnuts
3 large eggs, lightly beaten
1 cup grated cheddar cheese
½ teaspoon celery salt
¾ cup finely chopped onion

¼ teaspoon garlic powder
½ teaspoon black pepper
3 cups whole wheat bread
  crumbs (approximately 6
  slices of bread, crumbled)*

Topping

¼ cup Bulls-eye original-flavor
  barbecue sauce or favorite
  brand

(continued)

*If necessary, add more bread crumbs a tablespoon at a time to make a firm loaf.

1. Preheat the oven to 350 degrees. Coat a 9 × 5 × 3-inch loaf pan with nonstick cooking spray.

2. In a medium bowl, combine all the loaf ingredients. Mix well.

3. Place the loaf mixture into the prepared pan and press the mixture firmly and evenly in the pan. Spread the barbecue sauce over the top of the loaf.

4. Cook uncovered for 45 minutes, or until the top and sides are browned well. Remove from the oven and let it sit for 5 minutes before turning out onto a serving platter. Cut into slices with a sharp or serrated edged knife and serve.

The Loaf with Heart (Artichoke Loaf)

---•---

WMHQ Test Kitchens

WMHQ Note: This is delicious served for lunch or as a side dish.

SERVES 6

Loaf

2 10-ounce packages frozen
    artichoke hearts
1½ tablespoons butter
1 medium onion, finely
    chopped
1 garlic clove, chopped
½ red bell pepper, finely
    chopped

4 large eggs, lightly beaten
1 cup heavy cream
½ cup grated Parmesan cheese
¼ teaspoon grated nutmeg
½ teaspoon salt
½ teaspoon white pepper

Thyme Mayonnaise

1 cup mayonnaise

1 teaspoon dried thyme, or 2
    teaspoons fresh

Optional Garnish

Thyme sprigs

(*continued*)

1. Preheat the oven to 350 degrees. Lightly oil a 9 × 5 × 3-inch loaf pan.

2. In a blender or food processor, finely chop the artichoke hearts.

3. In a large skillet, melt the butter and sauté the onion, garlic, and red bell pepper until tender, about 4 to 6 minutes. Set aside to cool.

4. In a large bowl, combine the eggs, cream, Parmesan cheese, nutmeg, salt, and white pepper. Add the vegetable mixture and chopped artichokes, and mix thoroughly. Pour the mixture into the prepared pan.

5. Place the loaf pan in a roasting pan and fill with hot water until it reaches halfway up the sides of the loaf pan. Bake for 30 minutes, or until a knife inserted in the center of the loaf comes out clean.

6. Mix the mayonnaise with the thyme.

7. Let the loaf sit for 10 minutes. Run a knife along the sides of the loaf to separate it from the pan and turn it out onto a serving platter. Garnish with fresh thyme and serve with thyme mayonnaise either on top of each slice or on the side.

Wild Rice Loaf

———————•———————

WMHQ Test Kitchens

WMHQ Note: Wild rice is not a rice at all but a grainlike seed of an aquatic grass cultivated in Minnesota, Wisconsin, and neighboring parts of Canada. Its firm texture makes the perfect loaf. —*T. K. Woods*

Serves 4

½ cup wild rice
½ cup dry white wine
1½ cups water
1 teaspoon salt
2 tablespoons olive oil
½ cup chopped celery
1 medium onion, chopped
2 large eggs, lightly beaten
2 tablespoons sherry

1 tablespoon Worcestershire
  sauce
1 cup grated sharp cheddar
  cheese or Velveeta
1 cup herb-seasoned dry
  stuffing*
½ cup slivered almonds,
  toasted

1. Preheat the oven to 325 degrees. Lightly coat a 7½ × 3 × 2½-inch loaf pan with nonstick cooking spray.

2. Wash the rice thoroughly. In a large saucepan, combine the wine, water and salt and bring to a boil. Add the rice, reduce the heat, cover, and simmer for 45 to 60 minutes or until the rice has puffed and most of the liquid has been absorbed. Fluff rice with a fork and cook uncovered to evaporate any excess liquid. This will make 2 cups of rice.

3. In a skillet, heat the olive oil and sauté the celery and onion until the onion is translucent, about 3 minutes. Remove and set aside to cool.

4. In a large bowl, combine the eggs, sherry, and Worcestershire sauce. Add the rice, cheddar cheese, stuffing mix, and almonds and blend thoroughly. If the mixture is too wet, add more stuffing a handful at a time until mixture is firmer.

5. Place the mixture in the prepared pan.

6. Cover the pan with aluminum foil and bake for 30 minutes. Remove the foil and cook 10 to 15 minutes longer for the top to brown, or until done. Let it sit for 10 minutes and turn out of the pan onto a serving platter.

*If necessary, add more stuffing a tablespoon at a time to make a firm loaf.

Chapter 9

Meat and Poultry Loaves by the Professionals

When we held the 1991 Northeast Regional Cookoff, we invited local restaurants and food service professionals to join us. A large booth was set up in the middle of the Hartford Civic Center, and the professional chefs sold their meatloaves for $1 a slice. All the money collected was donated to Food Share, a Hartford area food bank. The recipes in this section came from the people and companies who took the time to help out.

There's quite a lot of variety in this group of recipes. If you've never tried a lamb loaf, see Marie-Christiane Corbett's winning recipe (page 256). The layer of sausage and onions between two layers of lamb is incredible!

You'll also find an excellent Nacho Loaf (page 250), poultry loaves, and even one that includes pumpkin. Give them a try. Even the ones with a lot of ingredients are presented in easy-to-follow steps.

1991 GRAND PRIZE—THE GREAT AMERICAN MEATLOAF CONTEST, PRO CHALLENGE

International Melting Pot Meatloaf

●

CANDIDO MARQUES

Executive Chef

Saint Francis Hospital

HARTFORD, CONNECTICUT

WMHQ Note: Since this is such a large recipe, you can use several loaf pans. Cook them all or freeze a few for future dinners. You can cut the recipe in half if you're not expecting 30 for dinner!

SERVES 30

1 pound French bread, crumbled*

6 large eggs, lightly beaten

2 cups tomato puree

4 pounds ground beef

4 pounds ground veal

1 cup sliced carrots

¾ cup diced Spanish onion

4 garlic cloves, crushed

½ cup tamari (or soy sauce)

1 tablespoon salt

¾ cup roasted and sliced fresh Mexican chilies (see page 115)

¼ cup chopped fresh Italian parsley

¼ teaspoon black pepper

1 pound choriso (spicy sausage), cut in strips

*If necessary, add more bread crumbs a tablespoon at a time to make a firm loaf.

1. Preheat the oven to 350 degrees. Lightly oil three or four 9 × 5 × 3-inch loaf pans, or a 10 × 13-inch roasting pan (to free-form 2 large loaves).

2. In a large bowl, combine the bread crumbs, eggs, and tomato puree. Mix well.

3. In another large bowl, combine the bread mixture with all the remaining ingredients except the sausage.

4. Layer each pan in the following order: meat mixture, sausage, meat mixture, sausage, meat mixture.

5. Bake for 1½ to 2 hours, or until done. Let the loaves sit for 10 minutes before serving.

Lunch Lady Liz's Mystery Meatloaf

————— • —————

LIZ LUCAS

Chef, The Watkinson School
HARTFORD, CONNECTICUT

WMHQ Note: As a chef at a prep school, Liz is used to cooking for large crowds. During the fund-raising 1991 contest, Liz made enough of this delicious meatloaf to serve hundreds.

SERVES 6

Loaf

3 tablespoons butter
1 large onion, finely diced
1 green bell pepper, finely diced
1 large celery stalk, finely diced
1 teaspoon dried thyme
1 pound ground veal

1 pound ground pork
½ pound ground beef
½ cup rolled oats*
⅓ cup barbecue sauce
2 large eggs, lightly beaten
2 teaspoons salt
1½ teaspoons black pepper

Topping

⅓ cup barbecue sauce

*If necessary, add more oats a tablespoon at a time to make a firm loaf.

1. Preheat the oven to 350 degrees. Lightly oil a 9 × 13-inch baking dish.

2. In a large skillet, melt the butter and sauté the onion, bell pepper, celery, and thyme until the vegetables are soft, about 4 to 6 minutes. Cool to room temperature.

3. In a large bowl, combine the cooked vegetables and meats. Add the oats, barbecue sauce, eggs, salt, and pepper. Mix well.

4. Press the mixture into the prepared baking dish. Spread the barbecue sauce on the loaf.

5. Bake for 1 hour or until done. Let the loaf sit for 10 minutes before serving.

Mamma's Own Meatloaf

———————•———————

Brian Reynolds

Manager, Canteen Corporation Corporate Caterers
MIDDLETOWN, CONNECTICUT

WMHQ Note: Being a corporate caterer, Brian is an expert at putting to-gether everything from quick lunches to fancy dinner parties. This recipe could be served at either.

Serves 8 to 10

3 pounds ground beef
1 pound ground pork
½ teaspoon ground cumin
¼ teaspoon cayenne pepper
¼ cup heavy cream
1 teaspoon chopped fresh
    parsley
⅓ cup milk

2 large eggs, lightly beaten
¼ cup molasses
4 tablespoons Dijon mustard
¾ cup diced red onion
2 garlic cloves, minced
4 drops hot sauce
¼ cup grated Romano cheese
¼ cup rye bread crumbs*

1. Preheat the oven to 350 degrees. Lightly oil two 9 × 5 × 3-inch loaf pans.

2. In a large bowl, combine all the ingredients and mix well.

3. Place the mixture in the prepared pans.

4. Bake for 1½ to 2 hours or until done. Let the loaves sit for 10 minutes before slicing.

*If necessary, add more bread crumbs a tablespoon at a time to make a firm loaf.

Louie's Meatloaf

●

LOUIE SLOVES

Owner, Louie's Westside Cafe
AMSTERDAM AVENUE, NEW YORK CITY

WMHQ Note: Louie Sloves wins the prize for driving the longest distance to help our food drive. Her restaurant in New York has been around since 1985 and is a real neighborhood favorite.

SERVES 8

2 tablespoons butter
½ cup chopped onion
½ cup chopped red bell
  pepper
½ cup chopped green bell
  pepper
½ cup chopped celery
¾ cup milk
2 cups plain bread crumbs*
2 pounds ground beef

⅓ cup ketchup
1 tablespoon soy sauce
2 tablespoons Worcestershire
  sauce
¼ teaspoon garlic powder
2 large eggs, lightly beaten
5 drops hot sauce
⅛ teaspoon salt
⅛ teaspoon black pepper

1. Preheat the oven to 350 degrees. Lightly oil a 9 × 5 × 3-inch loaf pan.

2. In a large skillet, melt the butter and sauté the onion, red pepper, green pepper, and celery until soft, about 4 to 6 minutes. Set aside to cool.

(continued)

*If necessary, add more bread crumbs a tablespoon at a time to make a firm loaf.

3. In a large bowl, combine the milk and bread crumbs. Mix well.

4. Add the vegetable mixture, remaining ingredients, and ground beef to the moistened bread crumbs and blend well.

5. Place the mixture in the prepared pan and bake for 1¼ hours or until done. Let the loaf sit for 10 minutes before slicing.

Turkey Loaf

•

LOUIE SLOVES

Owner, Louie's Westside Cafe
AMSTERDAM AVENUE, NEW YORK CITY

WMHQ Note: It was Louie's Turkey Loaf that helped us decide to include a poultry category for the 1992 contest. When she served this recipe during the Meatloaf Weekend, people stood in line twice to get more of it!

SERVES 6 to 8

Loaf

½ cup cooked rice*
2 pounds ground turkey
¼ cup milk
½ teaspoon fresh thyme
½ tablespoon chopped fresh
  parsley

2 tablespoons mayonnaise
2 large egg whites
⅛ teaspoon salt
⅛ teaspoon white pepper
½ cup water

*If necessary, add more rice a tablespoon at a time to make a firm loaf.

Topping

2 tablespoons butter

1. Preheat the oven to 350 degrees. Lightly oil a 9 × 13-inch baking dish.

2. In a food processor or blender, puree the cooked rice. Place the rice in a large bowl.

3. To the rice, add all the remaining ingredients except the water, and mix well.

4. Form the mixture into a loaf and place in the prepared baking dish. Dot the top of the loaf with the butter. Pour the water around the turkey loaf and cover with foil. Bake for 1 hour or until done. Let the loaf sit for 10 minutes before slicing.

Nacho Loaf

———————•———————

SUSAN HARGER

Pastry Chef, Hemingway's Collins Plaza
CEDAR RAPIDS, IOWA

WMHQ Note: The cheese sauce in this recipe can be used in a lot of other ways. It's great on nacho chips or vegetables. You can easily double the cheese sauce recipe and freeze it for future use.

When any sauce calls for milk, it's a good idea to have it at room temperature or slightly warm before adding it to the rest of the sauce. This will make the consistency smoother and avoid those dreaded lumps.

SERVES 6

Loaf

2 pounds lean ground beef
½ cup sour cream
1 cup shredded cheddar cheese
½ cup diced onion
½ cup mild salsa (hotter, if
    you prefer)

½ cup cornmeal*
1 envelope (1¼ ounces) taco
    seasoning
1 2¼-ounce can black olives,
    sliced

Cheese Sauce

2 tablespoons margarine
2 tablespoons flour
3 drops hot sauce

1 cup milk
1 cup shredded cheddar cheese
⅛ teaspoon salt

*If necessary, add more cornmeal a tablespoon at a time to make a firm loaf.

1. Preheat the oven to 350 degrees. Lightly oil a 9 × 5 × 3-inch loaf pan.

2. In a large bowl, combine all the loaf ingredients except the olives, and mix well. Gently work the sliced olives into the mixture.

3. Press the meat mixture into the prepared pan.

4. Bake for 1 hour or until done. Remove from the oven and drain off any liquid. Let the loaf sit for 10 minutes before serving.

5. While the loaf is baking, in a small saucepan melt the margarine. Add the flour and hot sauce and blend well. Cook for 1 minute, stirring constantly.

6. Add the milk all at once, mixing well. Keep stirring until the mixture starts to boil and thicken. Remove from the heat and add the cheese all at once. Stir until the cheese is melted and then salt as needed.

7. Serve the cheese sauce over the nacho loaf. Garnish with chips and jalapeño peppers.

Santa Fe Turkey Loaf

———————•———————

GUS STICKLEY

Self-employed food professional
HARWICHPORT, MASSACHUSETTS

WMHQ Note: This is a very flavorful turkey (or chicken) loaf. Gus did a wonderful job giving this simple-to-prepare loaf an interesting blend of spices and flavors.

SERVES 6 to 8

Loaf

4 tablespoons butter
1 celery stalk, diced
½ medium Spanish onion, diced
½ green bell pepper, diced
½ red bell pepper, diced
1 tablespoon garlic, minced
1½ cups canned corn kernels
1 4-ounce can mild green chilies, chopped, or jalapeño peppers to taste

15 to 20 large ripe olives, roughly chopped
2 pounds ground turkey or chicken
1 teaspoon black pepper
2 teaspoons salt
1 teaspoon hot sauce
¾ cup plain bread crumbs*
½ cup barbecue sauce
2 large eggs, lightly beaten

Topping

⅓ to ½ cup barbecue sauce

---

*If necessary, add more bread crumbs a tablespoon at a time to make a firm loaf.

1. Preheat the oven to 325 degrees. Lightly oil a 9 × 5 × 3-inch loaf pan.

2. In a large skillet, melt the butter and sauté the celery, onion, bell peppers, and garlic until just tender, about 4 to 6 minutes.

3. Add the corn, chilies, and olives and sauté for a few minutes. Cool and set aside.

4. In a large bowl, combine all the remaining ingredients. Add the sautéed vegetables and mix thoroughly.

5. Form the mixture into a loaf and spread the barbecue sauce on top.

6. Bake for 1 hour or until done. Let the loaf sit for 15 minutes before slicing.

Santa Fe Stuffed Meatloaf

•

KAREN MARTIS

Editor and Publisher, COOKING CONTEST CHRONICLE

MERRILLVILLE, INDIANA

"I created this recipe using leftover canned pumpkin and refried beans. This is the first time that I used cornbread crumbs in any recipe. The total result was *great*! I sometimes substitute hickory-flavored barbecue sauce in place of salsa."

—KAREN MARTIS

WMHQ Note: Karen is one of those friends we've never met . . . except on the phone. She publishes the Cooking Contest Chronicle. *We didn't realize how many cooking contests there are every year until we began receiving her newsletter.*

SERVES 6

1 pound ground beef
¾ pound ground veal
1½ cups fresh cornbread, crumbled*
1 large egg, lightly beaten
⅓ cup chopped celery
1 teaspoon all-purpose herb and spice blend seasoning such as Bell's Herbs or Jane's Krazy Mixed Up Salt
⅛ teaspoon white pepper

1 cup canned pumpkin
½ cup chopped onion
2 garlic cloves, minced
½ teaspoon salt
¾ cup canned refried beans
1 4-ounce package cream cheese, softened
½ cup shredded sharp cheddar cheese
⅓ cup chunky salsa

*If necessary, add more cornbread crumbs a tablespoon at a time to make a firm loaf.

1. Preheat the oven to 325 degrees. Lightly oil a 9 × 5 × 3-inch loaf pan.

2. In a large bowl, combine the ground beef, veal, cornbread crumbs, egg, celery, herb and spice blend, white pepper, pumpkin, onion, garlic, and salt.

3. Place half the mixture in the prepared pan.

4. In a small bowl, combine the beans and cream cheese. Using an electric mixer on low, blend ingredients until smooth, or mix by hand.

5. Spread the mixture to cover the meat completely. Top with the cheddar cheese.

6. Place the remaining meatloaf mixture on top of the cheddar cheese. Top the loaf with salsa.

7. Bake uncovered for 30 minutes. Cover with foil and bake 30 minutes more, or until done. Drain the drippings and let the loaf sit for 10 minutes. Serve, if desired, with a tomato sauce or additional salsa.

Queen of Sheba Meatloaf

MARIE-CHRISTIANE G. CORBETT

Private Caterer Cook
Aetna Institute
HARTFORD, CONNECTICUT

"Surround your loaf with sautéed green beans and almond slivers, and garnish with small cherry tomatoes and Kalamata olives. Serve with Red Bliss potatoes, salad greens, and a glass of Ouzo."
　　　　　　　　　　　　　　　　　　—MARIE-CHRISTIANE G. CORBETT

SERVES 8 to 10

2 tablespoons virgin olive oil
3 tablespoons butter
4 garlic cloves, crushed
2 medium onions, finely
　chopped
½ cup finely chopped fresh
　Italian parsley
1 teaspoon fennel seeds
2½ pounds lean ground lamb

1 pound ground hot sausage,
　casing removed
Juice of 1 lime
¼ cup dry vermouth
¾ cup fine bulgur wheat,
　soaked for 30 minutes in
　water to cover*
2 large eggs, lightly beaten
3 tablespoons ketchup

*If necessary, add more bulgur a tablespoon at a time to make a firm loaf.

1 teaspoon sesame oil
2 tablespoons dried mint
1 teaspoon ground allspice
¼ teaspoon dried rosemary
1 teaspoon ground cinnamon
½ teaspoon grated nutmeg

⅛ teaspoon black pepper
2 tablespoons Worcestershire
  sauce
⅓ cup toasted pine nuts
⅓ cup pistachios
3 bay leaves, split in half

1. Preheat the oven to 375 degrees. Thoroughly coat a Bundt pan with olive oil.

2. In a large sauté pan, heat the olive oil and 2 tablespoons of the butter. Add the garlic and onions. Sauté until the onions are translucent, about 3 minutes. Add the parsley and fennel seeds.

3. Remove half the onion mixture and combine with the ground lamb in a large bowl. Set the other half of the onion mixture aside.

4. Add the ground sausage to the sauté pan and brown. Add the lime juice and vermouth. Remove from the heat. Add this mixture to the reserved onion mixture. Set aside.

5. Squeeze the excess water from the bulgur wheat. Mix with the lamb. Add the eggs, ketchup, sesame oil, mint, allspice, rosemary, cinnamon, nutmeg, black pepper, and Worcestershire sauce. Mix well. Divide this mixture in half.

6. Press half the lamb mixture into the pan. Arrange the sausage mixture on top of the lamb. Sprinkle the pine nuts and pistachios evenly over the sausage layer.

7. Press the other half of the lamb mixture on top of the nut layer. Dot the loaf with the remaining tablespoon of butter and place the broken bay leaves on top of the loaf.

8. Bake for 1 hour or until done. Remove the bay leaves. Let the loaf sit for 15 minutes before inverting it onto a round serving platter.

Smooth as Silk Turkey Loaf

·

STEPHEN KILBRIDE
Pastry Chef, The 1848 Restaurant
MARIETTA, GEORGIA

"The loaf may be sliced and served immediately. Tomato sauce is a fine accompaniment. This loaf may also be served chilled and sliced very thin for sandwiches and party platters."
—STEPHEN KILBRIDE

SERVES 4 to 6

1½ tablespoons olive oil
½ medium onion, diced
1½ pounds ground turkey
6 large fresh basil leaves,
  diced, or 1 teaspoon dried
2 tablespoons chopped fresh
  parsley
2 tablespoons ketchup

1 tablespoon grated Parmesan
  cheese
⅛ teaspoon salt
⅛ teaspoon black pepper
2 large eggs, lightly beaten
1½ cups seasoned bread
  crumbs*

1. Preheat the oven to 350 degrees. Lightly oil a 9 × 5 × 3-inch loaf pan.

2. In a skillet, heat the olive oil and sauté the onion until translucent, about 3 minutes. Do not let it get brown.

3. In a large bowl, combine all the ingredients except the bread crumbs, and mix thoroughly.

4. Add the bread crumbs just to the point where the mixture can be shaped. The loaf should still be slightly wet.

5. Place the mixture in the prepared pan and cover with aluminum foil.

6. Bake for 1 hour or until done.

*If necessary, add more bread crumbs a tablespoon at a time to make a firm loaf.

Chapter 10

Meatloaves Created by Family, Friends, and the Test Kitchens of World Meatloaf Headquarters

*T*he recipes in this section were given to us by friends and family or were developed in our test kitchens.

Quite often, we were left with extra ingredients after making twenty or thirty meatloaves a day. Instead of throwing out half-empty jars of ingredients, we used them to develop new recipes. As with all the recipes in this book, they were tested and sampled by meatloaf enthusiasts and WMHQ staff members.

One day T. K. and I had a competition: Who could make the best loaf with the leftovers on the counter? We ran around the kitchen, grabbing different ingredients and incorporating them into an edible loaf. Fortunately, you won't find T. K.'s Tuna, Bacon, Jalapeño, Rye Bread, Onion, Black Bean, and Alfalfa Sprout Loaf in this book.

Upside-Down Pineapple Ham Loaf

———•———

WMHQ TEST KITCHENS

WMHQ Note: This is a great way to use leftover ham. Ham is salty, so we have combined spices, brown sugar, and pineapple to help balance the salty flavor.

For variety, spice the loaf as you would spice a whole ham. The pineapple rings provide decoration, but you can also use crushed pineapple if you prefer.

SERVES 6

1 pound boneless cooked ham
2 large eggs, lightly beaten
1 tablespoon spicy brown
   mustard
½ teaspoon ground cloves
1 teaspoon black pepper

1 8-ounce can pineapple rings,
   drained and juice reserved
¼ cup grated onion
1¼ cups plain bread crumbs*
½ cup light brown sugar,
   packed

*If necessary, add more bread crumbs a tablespoon at a time to make a firm loaf.

1. Preheat the oven to 350 degrees. Thoroughly oil a 9 × 5 × 3-inch loaf pan.

2. In a food processor, grind the cooked ham to a fine texture.

3. In a large bowl, combine the eggs, mustard, cloves, black pepper, pineapple juice, and grated onion.

4. Add the ground ham and mix well. Add bread crumbs.

5. Place 3 or 4 pineapple rings on the bottom of the pan. Sprinkle the pineapple with the brown sugar. Press the ham loaf mixture on top of the brown sugar and pineapple rings.

6. Bake for 1½ hours or until done.

7. Remove the loaf from the oven and let it sit for 10 to 15 minutes. Run a knife along the sides of the pan to separate the loaf from the sides. Carefully turn the loaf onto a large flat serving platter and scrape any juices left in the pan onto the loaf.

Lyle's Châteauneuf-du-"Pop" Loaf

---•---

WMHQ TEST KITCHENS

"My father taught me the appreciation of fine wines. As a little girl, we had fun pronouncing the name of this wine, which he often selected to accompany a roast or a steak at dinner, so this loaf is dedicated to my Pop." —T. K. WOODS

WMHQ Note: There is a theory floating out there that it doesn't matter what quality wine you cook with because it cooks out anyway. We'd like to swat that theory with this important fact: Almost all the alcohol in wine cooks out, but the flavor *remains. Since the flavor of this loaf is predominantly the burgundy wine, the quality of wine you use will enhance the taste of the loaf. We're not suggesting you use a $30 bottle. A bottle of Châteauneuf-du-Pape priced under $15 will work well, and then you can serve it as the accompanying wine with your meatloaf dinner.*

SERVES 6 to 8

Meatloaf

1 tablespoon butter
2 garlic cloves, minced
½ cup sliced scallions
   (including green part)
2 large eggs, lightly beaten
¼ cup ketchup

1 teaspoon celery salt
1 teaspoon black pepper
½ cup Châteauneuf-du-Pape
   or Merlot
2 pounds lean ground beef
1 cup plain bread crumbs*

---

*If necessary, add more bread crumbs a tablespoon at a time to make a firm loaf.

Sauce

2 scallions, finely chopped
½ cup Châteauneuf-du-Pape
  or Merlot

1 beef bouillon cube dissolved
  in 1 cup boiling water
¼ teaspoon black pepper

1. Preheat the oven to 350 degrees. Lightly oil a 9 × 5 × 3-inch loaf pan.

2. In a skillet, melt the butter and sauté the garlic and scallions until translucent, about 3 minutes. Let the mixture cool.

3. In a large bowl, combine the eggs, ketchup, celery salt, black pepper, and wine. Add the sautéed garlic and scallions.

4. Add the beef and bread crumbs and thoroughly mix the ingredients.

5. Place the meatloaf mixture in the prepared pan and bake for 1 hour. Remove the loaf from the oven and drain the drippings into a small bowl. Return the loaf to the oven for another 30 minutes or until done. Let the loaf sit for 10 minutes before serving.

6. While the loaf cools, prepare the sauce. In a skillet, place 3 tablespoons of drippings. Over medium heat, sauté the scallions in the drippings until translucent, about 3 minutes. Reduce the heat to low and add the wine, broth, and black pepper. Let the mixture simmer for 20 minutes.

7. Spoon some of the sauce on each slice of meatloaf and serve the remaining sauce in a gravy boat.

Beef Strogaloaf

———————————•———————————

WMHQ Test Kitchens

WMHQ Note: We have found that when you use milk, cream, or sour cream in a sauce or gravy, it is best to remove it from the refrigerator as you start the recipe, so that it will be at room temperature by the time you make the sauce or gravy. It will blend more easily if at room temperature.

Serves 6

Meatloaf

2 tablespoons butter
2 tablespoons olive oil
1 garlic clove, minced
½ cup chopped celery
½ cup chopped onion
1 cup sliced fresh mushrooms
1½ pounds ground beef
2 large eggs, lightly beaten

1 cup plain bread crumbs*
¼ cup sour cream
1 tablespoon chopped fresh
   dill or 1 teaspoon dried
1 teaspoon salt
1 tablespoon Worcestershire
   sauce
½ teaspoon black pepper

Sour Cream Sauce

2 tablespoons butter
½ cup sliced fresh mushrooms
2 tablespoons flour
¼ cup dry white wine
½ teaspoon tomato paste
½ teaspoon salt
⅛ teaspoon black pepper

2 teaspoons chopped fresh dill
   or ½ teaspoon dried
½ cup cream (at room
   temperature)
½ cup sour cream (at room
   temperature)

*If necessary, add more bread crumbs a tablespoon at a time to make a firm loaf.

1. Preheat the oven to 350 degrees. Lightly oil a 9 × 5 × 3-inch loaf pan.

2. In a skillet, heat the butter and olive oil. Sauté the garlic, celery, and onion until the onion is translucent, about 3 minutes. Remove from the skillet and set aside to cool. In the same pan, sauté the mushrooms until they begin to brown, about 2 minutes. Remove and set aside to cool.

3. In a large bowl, combine all the remaining meatloaf ingredients. Add the sautéed vegetables and mix well.

4. Place the mixture in the prepared pan and bake for 1 hour or until done.

5. While the meatloaf cools, prepare the sauce. In a skillet on medium heat melt the butter and sauté the mushrooms for 4 minutes or until they begin to brown. Add the flour and cook stirring for 3 minutes.

6. Stir in the white wine, tomato paste, salt, black pepper, and dill to the mushroom mixture and simmer for 8 to 10 minutes.

7. Remove the skillet from the heat. Stir in the cream and the sour cream until it is smooth. Add more cream to thin the sauce or add more sour cream to thicken it. Correct seasoning by adding more salt and pepper. Serve the sauce over each slice of meatloaf or on the side.

8. Let the loaf sit for 10 minutes. Serve the meatloaf slices with the sour cream sauce on a bed of egg noodles.

Meatloaf Satay

———————•———————

WMHQ TEST KITCHENS

WMHQ Note: This meatloaf is delicious the next day. Serve cold or reheat slices and serve them in a pita pocket. Add alfalfa sprouts and drizzle some satay sauce on top.

SERVES 6

Meatloaf

1 pound ground beef
½ pound ground lamb
1 tablespoon peanut oil
2 large eggs, lightly beaten
1 cup plain bread crumbs*
1 garlic clove, minced
¼ cup ketchup
1 tablespoon ground coriander

1 tablespoon ground cumin
2 teaspoons turmeric
1 teaspoon curry powder, or
  more to taste
½ cup heavy cream
¼ cup coarsely chopped
  unsalted peanuts
¼ teaspoon salt

Satay Sauce

3 tablespoons peanut butter
2 tablespoons soy sauce
2 tablespoons sugar

Juice of 1 lime
½ cup grated onion
¼ cup water

1. Preheat the oven to 350 degrees. Lightly oil a 9 × 5 × 3-inch loaf pan.

*If necessary, add more bread crumbs a tablespoon at a time to make a firm loaf.

2. In a large bowl, combine all the meatloaf ingredients and mix well. Cover the bowl with plastic wrap or foil and refrigerate for at least 1 hour.

3. Remove the mixture from the refrigerator and place in the prepared pan. Bake for 1½ hours or until done.

4. In a saucepan, mix the sauce ingredients and simmer over low heat, stirring, until smooth and creamy. If the sauce is too thick, add more water until it reaches the desired consistency.

5. Let the loaf sit for 15 minutes. Slice and serve with warmed satay sauce on the side.

Soy What Loaf, Honey?

•

WMHQ Test Kitchens

WMHQ Note: The honey and water chestnuts give this simple-to-prepare loaf an exotic flavor. Fried rice would be the perfect accompaniment to this loaf.

Serves 6

1½ pounds ground beef
1 8-ounce can water chestnuts, coarsely chopped
½ cup soy sauce
½ cup honey

10 fresh basil leaves, chopped
½ teaspoon garlic powder
1 large egg, lightly beaten
1¼ cups plain bread crumbs*

(continued)

*If necessary, add more bread crumbs a tablespoon at a time to make a firm loaf.

1. Preheat the oven to 350 degrees. Lightly oil a 9 × 5 × 3-inch loaf pan.

2. In a large bowl, combine all the ingredients and mix well. Cover the bowl with aluminum foil or plastic wrap and refrigerate for 1 hour.

3. Place the mixture in the prepared pan and bake for 1 hour or until done. Let it sit for 10 minutes before serving.

Roasted Garlic Loaf

●

WMHQ TEST KITCHENS

WMHQ Note: Roasted garlic sounds exotic, but it is so easy to prepare. When recipes call for minced garlic cloves, try using roasted garlic, instead— it's delicious!

If you want to be real popular in your neighborhood, roast a few heads of garlic and open your kitchen window. The smell grabs people by their noses and yanks them right to your kitchen door. That's one of the best things about running a meatloaf contest—there's a meatloaf or two always lying around for unexpected company.

SERVES 6 to 8

Roasted Garlic Sauce

1 medium head garlic
1 tablespoon sour cream

2 tablespoons mayonnaise

Meatloaf

½ cup sour cream
¼ cup mayonnaise
1½ pounds lean ground beef
½ pound bulk sausage
2 teaspoons olive oil

1 teaspoon salt
1 cup crushed croutons*
½ cup whole croutons
1 large egg, lightly beaten

1. Preheat the oven to 375 degrees. Lightly oil a 9 × 5 × 3-inch loaf pan.

2. Cut off the top of the garlic head. Leaving it unpeeled, place it in a piece of aluminum foil. Drizzle the olive oil over the garlic. Close the foil and place in the oven for 45 minutes. The garlic is done when soft.

3. Remove 1 roasted garlic clove from its skin and set remainder aside for the loaf. With the back of a spoon mash the clove. Mix in a small bowl with the sour cream and mayonnaise. Set aside.

4. Over a large bowl, separate a clove from the garlic head by pinching the clove's end. The clove will slip from its skin easily. Repeat the process with each clove.

5. With the back of a large spoon, mash the roasted cloves. Stir in the sour cream and mayonnaise. Add the remaining ingredients and mix well.

6. Place the shaped meat mixture in the prepared pan. Bake for 45 minutes. Remove from the oven and spread the sauce on the loaf. Bake for 15 minutes more. To ensure the top browns, place the loaf under the broiler for a few minutes. Watch carefully.

7. Let the loaf sit for 10 minutes before slicing.

*If necessary, add more crouton crumbs a tablespoon at a time to make a firm loaf.

Meatloaf in a Pumpkin

———————•———————

BETSY PHELAN
AVON, CONNECTICUT

"This can be assembled early in the day and baked just before serving. If the pumpkin won't stand up straight, cut a small piece off the bottom to level it. I have brought this to the table whole, surrounded by small gourds and a flower or two."
—BETSY PHELAN

WMHQ Note: This recipe was developed by one of our best friends. Betsy was instrumental in the 1991 Great American Meatloaf Contest in Hartford. She, her daughter Keli, and her son Kevin (future World Cup soccer star) worked around the clock to ensure that the contest and weekend would be a success.

SERVES 8 to 10

1 small pumpkin, about 9 inches in diameter
2 teaspoons salt
2 teaspoons olive oil
2 pounds lean ground beef
1 pound ground ham
2½ cups finely chopped onions
1 green bell pepper, finely chopped

2 teaspoons dried oregano
1 teaspoon cider vinegar
1 teaspoon black pepper
¼ teaspoon garlic powder
1 cup raisins
1 cup peeled and chopped apple
1 8-ounce can tomato sauce
3 large eggs, lightly beaten

1. Preheat the oven to 350 degrees. Use a 9 × 13-inch baking dish.

2. Cut off the top of the pumpkin to use as a lid, then scrape the pumpkin clean of seeds and pulp.

3. Place the lid back on and put the pumpkin in a large pot. Cover with salted water and bring to a boil. Reduce the heat to low and simmer for 20 to 30 minutes or until the pumpkin is tender to the touch but still holds it shape firmly.

4. Drain, then salt the inside of the pumpkin. While the pumpkin is simmering, make the meatloaf.

5. In a large skillet, heat the olive oil and sauté the beef and ham with the onions and green bell pepper until the meat is brown and crumbly, about 4 to 6 minutes. Remove from the heat. To the sauté pan, add the rest of the ingredients except the eggs.

6. Stir the ingredients together, then cook over low heat, stirring occasionally for 4 minutes. Remove from the heat and cool for 10 minutes. Thoroughly mix in the eggs.

7. Pack the meat mixture firmly into the drained and salted pumpkin. Place the pumpkin lid on and put the pumpkin in the baking pan and bake for 1 hour or until done.

8. To serve, cut through the pumpkin shell into wedges, as both shell and filling can be eaten.

My Favorite Meatloaf

———————•———————

WMHQ Note: This is a loaf I've developed over the years to incorporate my favorite two meats: bacon and hot sausage. It's a simple loaf, it's filling, it's my favorite loaf!   —*Peter Kaufman*

SERVES 6 to 8

Meatloaf

1 pound lean ground beef
1 pound hot Italian sausage,
  casing removed
6 strips bacon, cooked,
  drained, and chopped
1 medium onion, diced
4 tablespoons ketchup

2 teaspoons spicy brown
  mustard
6 drops hot sauce
1 cup cornflake crumbs*
4 tablespoons Worcestershire
  sauce
4 tablespoons steak sauce

Topping

3 tablespoons cornflake
  crumbs

*If necessary, add more cornflake crumbs a tablespoon at a time to make a firm loaf.

1. Preheat the oven to 350 degrees. Lightly coat a cooling or roasting rack with nonstick spray. Line a 9 × 13-inch baking dish with aluminum foil.

2. In a large bowl, combine all the loaf ingredients and mix well.

3. Form the mixture into a loaf. Place on the prepared rack and set in the prepared pan. Sprinkle the crumbs on the top of the loaf.

4. Bake for 1 hour or until done. Broil the loaf for the last 5 minutes to brown the crumbs on top. Let the loaf sit for 10 minutes before slicing.

Stu's Pride and Loaf

———————————•———————————

WMHQ Note: Stu is my father. Growing up, we always had Wispride cheese in the house. It was a favorite snack, so I'm dedicating this Wispride cheese and Ritz cracker loaf to my dad. He told me that nobody had ever dedicated a meatloaf to him before. Who would have guessed?

—*Peter Kaufman*

SERVES 6 to 8

Filling

4 ounces Wispride cheese (or more if you'd like), at room temperature

12 Ritz crackers

Meatloaf

2 pounds lean ground beef
1 medium onion, chopped
½ celery stalk, chopped
¼ green bell pepper, chopped

3 tablespoons ketchup
1 tablespoon prepared yellow mustard
¾ cup crushed Ritz crackers*

1. Preheat the oven to 350 degrees. Lightly oil a 9 × 5 × 3-inch loaf pan.

2. Spread the cheese on the crackers so that it covers the crackers completely. Set them aside.

*If necessary, add more cracker crumbs a tablespoon at a time to make a firm loaf.

3. In a large bowl, combine the meatloaf ingredients. Add more crushed crackers if you want a firmer loaf.

4. Place half the meatloaf mixture in the prepared pan. Put the cheese and crackers (whole) as a layer on top of the meatloaf. Use all the crackers and cheese. Place the other half of the meat mixture on top of the cheese and crackers.

5. Bake for 1¼ hours or until done.

6. Let it sit for 10 minutes before slicing.

Tim's Diner Meatloaf with Biscuits

•

TIM M. BUIE

BOSTON, MASSACHUSETTS

"Biscuits and Gravy is a favorite combination, served in diners throughout the Midwest and the South."
                                                                              —TIM BUIE

WMHQ Note: Tim Buie is almost like a member of the family. You can't turn around in the WMHQ kitchen without running into him. He even gets his mail here!

SERVES 6 to 8

Meatloaf

1½ pounds lean ground beef
¾ pound ground sausage
1 medium onion, finely
    chopped
2 cups bread crumbs (fresh
    preferred)*

¼ cup sour cream
1 large egg, lightly beaten
1 teaspoon Liquid Smoke
    (available near the barbecue
    sauces in most grocery
    stores)

Gravy

¾ pound ground sausage
3 tablespoons all-purpose flour
3 tablespoons sour cream
1½ cups milk, at room
    temperature

¼ teaspoon salt
⅛ teaspoon black pepper

*If necessary, add more bread crumbs a tablespoon at a time to make a firm loaf.

Biscuits

1 package biscuit mix or
  Pillsbury Baking Powder
  Biscuits, depending on how
  many biscuits you want to
  make

1. Preheat the oven to 350 degrees. Lightly coat a cooling rack with nonstick cooking spray and place on an aluminum-foil-lined 10 × 13-inch roasting pan.

2. In a large bowl, combine the meatloaf ingredients and mix well.

3. Form the mixture into a round loaf. Place the loaf on the rack in the prepared roasting pan.

4. Bake for 1 hour or until done.

5. In a large skillet, brown the sausage. Drain and set aside the sausage, leaving 3 tablespoons of drippings in the skillet over medium-low heat.

6. Slowly stir in the flour and cook for 4 minutes.

7. Remove the skillet from the heat and stir in the sour cream.

8. Stir in the milk until the gravy has the consistency you desire.

9. Add the sausage, salt, and pepper.

10. Prepare the biscuits according to package instructions and bake 15 to 20 minutes before the meatloaf is done.

11. Let the loaf sit for 10 minutes before serving. Slice the meatloaf and serve on a large platter with the biscuits surrounding the loaf. Drizzle the gravy over the slices and serve extra gravy on the side.

T. K.'s In-the-Chips Meatloaf

———————————•———————————

WMHQ Note: T. K. loves potato chips. She developed this recipe when she realized that her beloved bag of potato chips had nothing left but a half-pound of crumbs.

SERVES 6 to 8

Meatloaf

2 pounds ground beef
1 medium onion, diced
¼ red bell pepper, diced
2 tablespoons ketchup

1 teaspoon spicy brown
   mustard
1 cup Italian-flavored bread
   crumbs*

Topping

½ teaspoon paprika

1½ cups crushed potato chips

1. Preheat the oven to 350 degrees. Lightly oil a 9 × 5 × 3-inch loaf pan.

2. In a large bowl, combine the meatloaf ingredients.

3. Form the mixture into a loaf.

4. On a large piece of wax paper, combine the paprika with the potato chips. Roll the loaf in the crushed chips to cover the entire loaf.

5. Bake the loaf for 1¼ hours or until done. Let the loaf sit for 10 minutes before slicing.

*If necessary, add more bread crumbs a tablespoon at a time to make a firm loaf.

Some Like It Hot Loaf

---•---

WMHQ TEST KITCHENS

WMHQ Note: This recipe was developed because some of us really love hot, hot food. If you're going to make this loaf, have plenty of cold beverages handy. Beer would work. And notify your next of kin.

SERVES 6 to 8

1½ pounds ground beef
½ pound hot sausage, casing
  removed
1 medium onion, chopped
2 tablespoons spicy brown
  mustard
2 jalapeño peppers, sliced
3 scallions, finely chopped
12 drops hot sauce
2 teaspoons cayenne pepper

2 teaspoons chili powder
1 large egg, lightly beaten
1 tablespoon soy sauce
1 tablespoon Worcestershire
  sauce
2 tablespoons ketchup
½ teaspoon salt
½ teaspoon black pepper
1 cup cornflake crumbs*

1. Preheat the oven to 350 degrees. Lightly oil a 9 × 5 × 3-inch loaf pan.

2. In a large mixing bowl, combine the meats well. Add the remaining ingredients and mix thoroughly.

3. Place the mixture in the prepared pan.

4. Bake for 1¼ hours or until done. Let the loaf sit for 10 minutes before slicing.

*If necessary, add more cornflake crumbs a tablespoon at a time to make a firm loaf.

Rondele Roll-Up

––––––––– • –––––––––

WMHQ TEST KITCHENS

WMHQ Note: This recipe was developed while we were in the middle of testing the roll-up recipes. Because Rondele cheese spreads so well, we thought it would be perfect to include in a meatloaf. And it is!

SERVES 6 to 8

Meatloaf

2 pounds lean ground beef
20 Carr crackers, crushed, or
    any other firm cracker*
1 medium onion, chopped
2 scallions, finely chopped

2 tablespoons ketchup
1 teaspoon prepared mustard
½ teaspoon salt
⅛ teaspoon black pepper

Filling

6 ounces Rondele cheese,
    softened

1 tablespoon milk

1. Preheat the oven to 350 degrees. Lightly coat a cooling or roasting rack with nonstick cooking spray and place on a foil-lined baking sheet with sides.

*If necessary, add more crushed crackers a tablespoon at a time to make a firm loaf.

2. In a large bowl, combine the meatloaf ingredients and mix well.

3. On a lightly oiled piece of aluminum foil which has been placed on a cookie sheet, press the meatloaf mixture into a rectange so it is a ½ inch thick. (See roll-up instructions on page 94.)

4. Cover the meat mixture with foil or plastic wrap and refrigerate for 30 minutes.

5. In a small bowl, combine the cheese and milk and mix until smooth.

6. Spread the cheese evenly over the meatloaf mixture. Leave a 1½-inch margin around the edges of the loaf. Beginning at the short side and using the aluminum foil to guide, carefully roll the loaf. Seal the edges and sides with a little water.

7. Place on the prepared rack and bake for 1½ hours or until done. Let the loaf stand for 10 minutes before slicing.

Mom's Meatloaf

●

ROBERTA KAUFMAN
WEST HARTFORD, CONNECTICUT

WMHQ Note: This is the recipe that started my love for meatloaf. Mom would make this once a week as her mother made it for her when she was growing up. But it's not meatloaf that I most remember about my grandmother.

When we went to New York City to visit her and Grandpa, she had a great way of making sure that nobody woke them until 8:00 in the morning. She told my brother, sister, and me that the city didn't turn the gas on until 8:00 A.M. so we couldn't have breakfast until then. Sometime around my fifteenth birthday I grew suspicious. (You can't fool me all the time.) I made a few phone calls and found out the truth.

When I made this recipe on "Live with Regis and Kathie Lee" in 1992, Regis had tears in his eyes when he tasted it. Maybe it's because he liked it, or maybe because I had him taste four meatloaves in five minutes.

SERVES 6 to 8

Meatloaf

2 tablespoons butter
1 medium onion, diced
2 pounds lean ground beef
1 egg, beaten
4 tablespoons ketchup
4 tablespoons Dijon mustard
4 tablespoons steak sauce

4 tablespoons Worcestershire sauce
5 drops of hot sauce
½ teaspoon salt
½ teaspoon black pepper
½ cup cornflake crumbs*

*If necessary, add more cornflake crumbs a tablespoon at a time to make a firm loaf.

Topping

3 tablespoons cornflake
  crumbs

1. Preheat the oven to 350 degrees. Lightly oil a 9 × 5 × 3-inch loaf pan.

2. In a medium skillet, melt the butter and sauté the onion until translucent, about 3 minutes. Remove from the heat and set aside to cool.

3. In a large bowl, combine the meat and all other ingredients except crumbs and mix well.

4. Add the sautéed onion to the mixture. Then add the cornflake crumbs to reach the desired consistency; mix thoroughly.

5. Cover the meat with aluminum foil or plastic wrap and refrigerate for 1 hour.

6. Place the meat mixture in the prepared pan. Dust the top of the meatloaf with cornflake crumbs.

7. Bake for 1 hour or until done. During the last 5 minutes of cooking, broil the loaf to brown the crumbs. Let the loaf sit for 10 minutes before slicing.

Patty's Loaf Gone Wild

•

WMHQ Test Kitchens

WMHQ Note: Wild rice is really a grass, not a rice. This accounts for its firm and nutty texture. And since it's less mushy than other rices, it is great in a loaf. Wild rice is often cultivated by hand and therefore can be expensive far from its home of 10,000 lakes. But 1 cup wild rice will make approximately 4 cups cooked.

"I call Minnesota my home, but I don't call home enough, according to my parents, who live three hours north of Minneapolis. Memories of my mother's fabulous wild rice casserole inspired the idea for this loaf. A vegetarian Wild Rice Loaf is on page 238."   —*T. K. Woods*

Serves 6 to 8

½ cup wild rice
2 cups water
2 chicken bouillon cubes, or 2
    packets Herb-Ox reduced-
    sodium chicken bouillon
4 strips uncooked bacon
1 red onion, chopped
½ cup celery, chopped
½ pound Shiitake mushrooms,
    sliced

½ cup slivered almonds,
    toasted
1 teaspoon dried thyme
1 teaspoon dried sage
½ teaspoon salt
1 teaspoon lemon pepper
½ teaspoon poultry seasoning
½ cup dry white wine
2 large eggs, lightly beaten
1 pound ground beef
¼ cup plain bread crumbs*

*If necessary, add more bread crumbs a tablespoon at a time to make a firm loaf.

1. Preheat the oven to 350 degrees. Lightly coat a 9 × 5 × 3-inch loaf pan with nonstick cooking spray.

2. Thoroughly wash the wild rice. In a large saucepan, boil the water. Add the bouillon cubes and dissolve them. Place the wild rice in the boiling bouillon, reduce the heat and simmer covered for 45 to 60 minutes or until the rice puffs and the liquid is absorbed. Fluff the rice with a fork and cook uncovered until the liquid is evaporated. This should make 2 cups cooked wild rice.

3. In a skillet, cook the bacon until limp but not too crispy. Remove the bacon and drain. Chop the cooled bacon into bite-size pieces.

4. In 2 tablespoons of the bacon grease, sauté the scallions, celery, and sliced mushrooms until tender, 4 to 6 minutes.

5. Add the toasted almonds, salt, lemon pepper, poultry seasoning, thyme, sage, and wine to the vegetable mixture. Simmer over low heat for 5 to 10 minutes.

6. In a large bowl, combine the egg, ground beef, and wild rice. Add the vegetable mixture and bacon pieces and blend thoroughly. If the mixture is too wet, add the bread crumbs one tablespoon at a time until the mixture is firmer.

7. Place the meatloaf mixture in the prepared pan. Cover the pan with aluminum foil and bake for 45 minutes. Remove the foil and cook 15 minutes longer for the top to brown or until done. Let it sit for 10 minutes and turn out of the pan onto a serving platter.

Super Bowl Kielbasa Loaf

———•———

TIM M. BUIE

BOSTON, MASSACHUSETTS

WMHQ Note: Originally from Kansas City, Missouri, Dr. Buie is a pediatric gastroenterologist. An avid cook, Dr. Buie loves having friends over to test his latest creations. And with his lab background, he isn't afraid to experiment. This hearty loaf was developed with one goal in mind: to feed four poker-playing buddies without having to clean more than two dishes. He doesn't recommend this loaf for his patients, but prescribes this great "guy" loaf for Super Bowl parties.

SERVES 6 to 8

Meatloaf

1½ pounds lean ground beef
½ pound cooked ham, cubed
½ pound cooked kielbasa, cubed
2 cups bread crumbs*

2 large eggs, lightly beaten
1 medium onion, finely chopped
½ teaspoon garlic powder

Pineapple Pizzazz Sauce

¼ cup diced onion
1 tablespoon butter
1 10-ounce can crushed pineapple with juice

¾ cup light brown sugar, packed
1 ounce Triple Sec liqueur

*If necessary, add more bread crumbs a tablespoon at a time to make a firm loaf.

1. Preheat the oven to 350 degrees. Lightly coat a 9 × 13-inch baking dish with nonstick cooking spray.

2. In a large bowl, combine all the meatloaf ingredients and mix well.

3. Place the mixture in the prepared dish and shape into a loaf. Bake for 30 minutes.

4. While the meatloaf is cooking, make the sauce. Remove the meatloaf from the oven and drain off ¼ cup of the drippings. Set aside.

5. In a small skillet, sauté the onion in the butter until translucent. In a medium saucepan, combine the pineapple, brown sugar, and meatloaf drippings. Add the onion. Cook the mixture over low heat until thick and bubbling. Stir in the Triple Sec, and cook a few more minutes on low heat.

6. Remove the loaf from the oven and top it with the sauce. Place the loaf back in the oven for another 20 minutes or until done.

Chapter 11

Side Dishes to Serve with Meatloaf

*S*pecial meatloaves deserve memorable side dishes. From the kitchens at World Meatloaf Headquarters as well as from family and friends, we want to share these interesting and delicious side dishes for meatloaf.

Of course, there's a recipe for mashed potatoes! What goes better with meatloaf? But we've offered some variations that zip up the smashed spud.

Most diners appreciate a meatloaf served with gravy. Here also are some basic sauces you can serve with both meatloaves and poultry loaves. These sauces are easy to make and provide the foundation for you to be creative. Season them with a variety of spices. However, make sure you season the gravies or sauces to work with the meat or poultry loaf and not overwhelm it.

Basic Mashed Potatoes

WMHQ Note: If you're going to make mashed potatoes, make a lot. Everybody always wants seconds.

SERVES 6

2 teaspoons salt
6 large baking potatoes
½ teaspoon white pepper

4 tablespoons butter
1½ cups milk

1. Fill a large pot with water. Add the salt and bring to a boil.

2. To prevent browning of the peeled potatoes, fill a large bowl with ice water. Peel the potatoes and cut into ¾-inch cubes. Drop the cubes immediately into the ice water.

3. When all the potatoes are cubed, remove them from the ice water and place in the boiling water.

4. Boil the potatoes for 20 to 25 minutes, or until tender. Drain the potatoes in a colander and return the cooked potatoes to the same large pot, now empty.

5. Reduce the heat to medium and cook the potatoes for 1 minute to remove the excess moisture. Add the white pepper.

6. In a saucepan, place the butter and milk and cook over low heat to melt the butter.

7. With a potato masher, mash the potatoes and slowly add the warmed milk and butter. Continue mashing the potatoes until smooth. If you want to remove the lumps completely, mix with an electric beater on low speed until the lumps are removed. Don't overbeat the potatoes.

Garlic Mashed Potatoes

———————•———————

WMHQ Note: Here's an easy way to jazz up mashed potatoes.

S E R V E S 6

3 tablespoons olive oil
1 medium head of garlic,
  cloves peeled and minced

Basic Mashed Potatoes
(page 290)

1. In a skillet, heat the olive oil. Sauté the garlic until tender, about 4 to 6 minutes.

2. Add the sautéed garlic to the mashed potatoes. Mix in thoroughly.

Mashed Potatoes with Romano or Parmesan Cheese

———————•———————

S E R V E S 6

Basic Mashed Potatoes
(page 290)

½ cup freshly grated Parmesan
  or Romano cheese

After the potatoes have been thoroughly mashed, sprinkle on the grated cheese and mix well.

Roasted Garlic Mashed Potatoes

———————•———————

SERVES 6

1 medium head of garlic
1 teaspoon olive oil

Basic Mashed Potatoes
(page 290)

1. Preheat the oven to 375 degrees.

2. Cut off the top of the head of garlic and place it unpeeled on a piece of aluminum foil. Drizzle the olive oil over the garlic and wrap the foil completely around it.

3. Place the garlic in the oven and roast for 45 minutes. The garlic is done when it is very tender.

4. Remove the garlic head and let it cool. In a small bowl, separate the garlic cloves and pinch the end of each clove so that it slips from its skin into the bowl. With a fork, mash the garlic cloves.

5. Add the mashed cloves to the cooked potatoes. With a potato masher, mash well until thoroughly blended.

Stupendous Potatoes

———————————•———————————

WMHQ Note: These taters are quick to make and hard to resist. If you like your potatoes crunchy, broil them longer than the directions specify.

SERVES 6 to 8

4 large baking potatoes
1 medium onion, diced

3 tablespoons paprika
2 teaspoons garlic salt

1. Preheat the oven to 350 degrees.

2. In a food processor, slice the potatoes with their skins on, or slice them by hand.

3. Spread the potatoes on a microwave-safe plate and cook on High for 6 minutes in a full-wattage microwave. With a spatula turn the potatoes over and cook on High for another 6 minutes.

4. Lightly oil a baking sheet and spread the potatoes out as much as possible. Spread the diced onion on top and add half the garlic salt and half the paprika.

5. Bake for 10 minutes. With a spatula, turn the potatoes over and add the remaining garlic salt and paprika. Continue baking until the edges begin to get crispy, another 5 to 10 minutes.

6. Place potatoes in broiler and broil for a few minutes until golden brown.

Homemade Cornbread

———————•———————

ALICE "BABE" ECKERT

SIOUX CITY, IOWA

WMHQ Note: One of our most enthusiastic judges of the meatloaf contest was Dawn Bain. She and her husband, Denny, never missed a chance to help us out. This recipe comes from Dawn's grandmother, Alice Eckert. As Mrs. Eckert says, "The best food is easy food!"

SERVES 6

1¼ cups all-purpose flour
¾ cup yellow cornmeal
¼ cup light brown sugar,
    packed
2 teaspoons baking powder

1 cup milk
¼ cup vegetable oil
1 large egg, lightly beaten
1 cup honey

1. Preheat the oven to 400 degrees. Lightly grease a 9 × 5 × 3-inch loaf pan.

2. In a large bowl, mix all the dry ingredients well.

3. Stir in the milk, oil, and egg. Mix until just moistened, being careful to make sure that there are no brown sugar lumps. Place in the prepared pan.

4. Bake for 15 minutes or until the top starts to brown.

5. Remove the pan from the oven and drizzle the honey on top. Continue to bake for 10 to 15 minutes more, until a toothpick inserted in the center comes out clean. Serve the cornbread warm.

Red Beans

DAWN BAIN

BOSTON, MASSACHUSETTS

WMHQ Note: One Sunday evening, after tasting fifteen or twenty meatloaves, our guests put down their plates and said "All right, what's for dinner?" Fortunately, Dawn brought twenty pounds of this dish and served it with her homemade corn bread and white rice.

SERVES 6 to 8

1 pound dried red beans
2 ham hocks or 1 ham bone
with some meat
1 large onion, chopped
8 to 10 scallions, chopped
(including the green part)
½ cup chopped green bell
pepper
¼ cup chopped fresh parsley

4 tablespoons butter
2 bay leaves
1½ teaspoons cayenne pepper
½ pound sausage, casing
removed, cooked
1 celery stalk, chopped
2 strips bacon, uncooked, cut
into pieces

1. Wash and sort the beans. Place the beans in a large Dutch oven or pot and cover with water. Bring to a boil and let boil for 5 minutes. Remove the pot from the heat and let the beans soak overnight. (Make sure the beans are covered with water.)

2. The next day, place the bean pot over medium-low heat. Add the remaining ingredients and simmer at least 2 hours or until the beans are soft. Don't let beans get mushy.

Mashed Sweet Potatoes with Scallions

•

WMHQ Note: The burnt orange of sweet potatoes with green scallions adds color and a refreshing variation to ordinary mashed sweet potatoes.

SERVES 4 to 6

1 teaspoon salt
3 large sweet potatoes, peeled
   and cubed
1–2 tablespoons olive oil
½ cup chopped scallions
   (including green part)

1 cup milk
1 cup half-and-half
4 tablespoons butter
1 teaspoon grated nutmeg

1. Bring a large pot of water to a boil and add salt.

2. Place sweet potatoes in boiling water and boil for 15 to 20 minutes or until tender.

3. In a skillet, heat the olive oil and sauté the scallions until translucent, about 3 minutes.

4. When potatoes are tender, drain in a colander and return to the pot. Reduce the heat to medium and cook the potatoes for a few seconds to dry them. Add the milk, cream, and butter. Increase the heat and bring to a boil, then remove the pot from the heat.

5. With a potato masher or a large serving fork, mash the potato with the milk, cream, and butter. Add the nutmeg and scallions and mix into the mashed potatoes. Serve with additional butter and salt and pepper to taste.

Idyllic Brussels Sprouts

———————— • ————————

WMHQ Note: Toss this dressing over the hot vegetable. There's no need to pass the butter or salt with these side dishes. Vary the recipe using green beans, cooked carrots, or broccoli.

SERVES 4 to 6

Idyll Wild Dressing

¼ cup red wine vinegar
1 cup olive oil
¼ cup lemon juice
¼ cup light brown sugar,
    packed
½ teaspoon seasoned salt

½ teaspoon dry mustard
2 tablespoons chutney
½ teaspoon black pepper
1½ pounds small Brussels
    sprouts, cleaned and
    trimmed
2 garlic cloves, crushed
3 tablespoons chopped
    scallions

1. In a blender or a food processor, combine ingredients for dressing.

2. With a sharp paring knife, cut an *x* in the stem of each Brussels sprout. Place 2 tablespoons of the dressing, the garlic, and the scallions in a saucepan. Add the sprouts and cover with water.

3. Bring the sprouts to a boil. Lower the heat and simmer, partly covered, until sprouts are just tender, about 20 to 30 minutes. Don't let them overcook.

4. Transfer the hot sprouts to a serving bowl. Drizzle dressing over the sprouts and serve.

Broccoli Diane

———•———

DIANE COMPTON
HAMDEN, CONNECTICUT

WMHQ Note: We've known Diane for years, and when the call went out to pitch in for the meatloaf contest, Diane was right there. A true friend, she did all the jobs nobody else wanted to do. In addition to being an invaluable member of the Meatloaf staff, she is a wonderful and innovative cook.

SERVES 4

1 head of broccoli
¼ cup olive oil
3 garlic cloves, sliced
¼ teaspoon dried hot pepper
    flakes

½ teaspoon salt
½ teaspoon black pepper
Juice of 1 lemon

1. Separate the florets of broccoli and slice the stalks. Lightly steam both for a few minutes. Do not let the broccoli get soggy.

2. Heat the olive oil in a sauté pan and add the garlic. Cook for 1 minute, then add the broccoli.

3. Cook until tender. Add the pepper flakes, salt, pepper, and lemon juice. Sauté for 10 minutes or until all ingredients are well incorporated.

Cherry Tomato Sauté

———————•———————

DIANE COMPTON
HAMDEN, CONNECTICUT

1 pint cherry tomatoes, rinsed
¼ cup olive oil
3 garlic cloves, chopped

½ cup chopped fresh parsley
¼ cup chopped fresh basil

1. Sauté the garlic in olive oil for 2 minutes. Add the cherry tomatoes and cook for 3 minutes.

2. Add the parsley and basil and sauté another 3 minutes.

3. Serve immediately.

Idyllic Corn Relish

———————•———————

WMHQ Note: To accompany some of the spicier loaves, this vegetable relish is ideal.

SERVES 6

1 15-ounce can niblet corn
1 15-ounce can kidney beans
1 medium onion, finely
   chopped

1 medium red bell pepper,
   finely chopped
¾ to 1 cup Idyll Wild Dressing
   (page 297)

1. In a large bowl, combine all the ingredients. Use more dressing if needed, but you don't want the vegetables swimming in it.

2. Place in a covered container and refrigerate (best if used the next day). Serve cold with your hottest loaf.

Basic Brown Sauce

———•———

WMHQ Note: You can flavor this basic sauce by adding Worcestershire, wine, and a variety of ingredients to taste.

MAKES 1 CUP

1 cup boiling water
1 beef bouillon cube, crushed,
   or 1 packet Herb-Ox beef
   bouillon

2 tablespoons butter
2 tablespoons all-purpose flour
Salt and pepper

1. Dissolve the crushed bouillon cube in the boiling water.

2. In a skillet, melt the butter over low heat. Add the flour and stir until blended. Cook the flour for a few minutes, stirring.

3. Pour in the hot bouillon. Stirring constantly, cook the sauce until it comes to a boil.

4. The sauce should be thickened. Season to taste with salt and pepper.

Chicken Flavored Gravy

———————•———————

WMHQ Note: To enhance the flavor of this gravy, add poultry seasoning, white wine Worcestershire sauce, or white wine.

MAKES 1 CUP

1 cup boiling water
1 chicken bouillon cube,
  crushed, or 1 packet Herb-
  Ox chicken bouillon

2 tablespoons butter
2 tablespoons all-purpose flour
Salt and pepper

1. Dissolve the crushed bouillon cube in the boiling water.

2. In a skillet, melt the butter over low heat. Add the flour and stir until blended. Cook the flour for a few minutes, stirring.

3. Pour in the hot bouillon. Stirring constantly, cook the sauce until it comes to a boil.

4. The sauce should be thickened. Season to taste with salt and pepper.

Gravy Made from Loaf Drippings

———————•———————

WMHQ Note: When making the gravy from either meat or poultry loaves, to make a cream gravy instead of a brown gravy, substitute room-temperature heavy cream or milk for the water. Make sure that you remove the pan from the heat when adding the milk or cream.

3 to 4 tablespoons loaf
  drippings
3 to 4 tablespoons all-purpose
  flour
1½ cups water

Salt and pepper to taste
Seasonings of your choice

1. Approximately 15 minutes before the loaf is done, remove it from the oven. With a turkey baster or large spoon, remove some drippings. Return the loaf to the oven.

2. Place the drippings in a large skillet over medium-high heat. Add the flour and blend thoroughly. Cook the flour, stirring for a few minutes.

3. Add the hot water to the skillet, stirring constantly. Cook the sauce until it comes to a boil.

4. Adjust the thickness of the sauce by adding more water if necessary. Season the gravy with salt, pepper, or other seasonings to taste.

Index